UNITED NATIONS?

AROUND THE MANCHESTER UNITED WORLD IN 80 GAMES...

Tim Webber

KNOW THE SCORE BOOKS SPORTS PUBLICATIONS

CULT HEROES	Author	ISBN
CARLISLE UNITED	Paul Harrison	978-1-905449-09-7
CELTIC	David Potter	978-1-905449-08-8
CHELSEA	Leo Moynihan	1-905449-00-3
MANCHESTER CITY	David Clayton	978-1-905449-05-7
NEWCASTLE	Dylan Younger	1-905449-03-8
NOTTINGHAM FOREST	David McVay	978-1-905449-06-4
RANGERS	Paul Smith	978-1-905449-07-1
SOUTHAMPTON	Jeremy Wilson	1-905449-01-1
WEST BROM	Simon Wright	1-905449-02-X

MATCH OF MY LIFE	Editor	ISBN
BRIGHTON	Paul Camillin	978-1-84818-000-0
DERBY COUNTY	Nick Johnson	978-1-905449-68-2
ENGLAND WORLD CUP	Massarella & Moynihan	1-905449-52-6
EUROPEAN CUP FINALS	Ben Lyttleton	1-905449-57-7
FA CUP FINALS 1953-1969	David Saffer	978-1-905449-53-8
FULHAM	Michael Heatley	1-905449-51-8
IPSWICH TOWN	Mel Henderson	978-1-84818-001-7
LEEDS	David Saffer	1-905449-54-2
LIVERPOOL	Leo Moynihan	1-905449-50-X
MANCHESTER UNITED	Ivan Ponting	978-1-905449-59-0
SHEFFIELD UNITED	Nick Johnson	1-905449-62-3
STOKE CITY	Simon Lowe	978-1-905449-55-2
SUNDERLAND	Rob Mason	1-905449-60-7
WOLVES	Simon Lowe	1-905449-56-9

PLAYER BY PLAYER	Author	ISBN
LIVERPOOL	Ivan Ponting	978-1-84818-306-3
MANCHESTER UNITED	Ivan Ponting	978-1-84818-500-1
TOTTENHAM HOTSPUR	Ivan Ponting	978-1-84818-501-8

GREATEST GAMES	Author	ISBN
SCOTLAND	David Potter	978-1-84818-200-4
SUNDERLAND	Rob Mason	978-1-84818-204-2
WEST BROM	Simon Wright	978-1-84818-206-6

GENERAL FOOTBALL	Author	ISBN
A GREAT FACE FOR RADIO	John Anderson	978-1-84818-403-9
A SMASHING LITTLE FOOTBALL FIRM	Nicky Allt	978-1-84818-402-2
BEHIND THE BACK PAGE	Christopher Davies	978-1-84818-506-7
BOOK OF FOOTBALL OBITUARIES	Ivan Ponting	978-1-905449-82-2
FORGIVE US OUR PRESS PASSES	Football Writers' Association	978-1-84818-507-4
JUST ONE OF SEVEN	Denis Smith	978-1-84818-504-3
MANCHESTER UNITED MAN & BABE	Wilf McGuinness	978-1-84818-503-6
NEVER HAD IT SO GOOD	Tim Quelch	978-1-84818-600-2
NO SMOKE, NO FIRE	Dave Jones	978-1-84818-513-5
NORTHERN AND PROUD	Paul Harrison	978-1-84818-505-0
OUTCASTS: The Lands That FIFA Forgot	Steve Menary	978-1-905449-31-6
PALLY	Gary Pallister	978-1-84818-500-5
PARISH TO PLANET	Eric Midwinter	978-1-905449-30-9
PLEASE MAY I HAVE MY FOOTBALL BACK?	Eric Alexander	978-1-84818-508-1
TACKLES LIKE A FERRET	Paul Parker	1-905449-46-1
THE DOOG	Harrison & Gordos	978-1-84818-502-9
THE RIVALS GAME	Douglas Beattie	978-1-905449-79-8
UNITED NATIONS?	Tim Webber	978-1-84818-405-3
WARK ON	John Wark	978-1-84818-511-1

RUGBY LEAGUE	Author	ISBN
MOML LEEDS RHINOS	Caplan & Saffer	978-1-905449-69-9
MOML WIGAN WARRIORS	David Kuzio	978-1-905449-66-8

CRICKET	Author	ISBN
ASHES TO DUST	Graham Cookson	978-1-905449-19-4
GROVEL!	David Tossell	978-1-905449-43-9
KP: CRICKET GENIUS?	Wayne Veysey	978-1-84818-701-6
MOML: THE ASHES	Pilger & Wightman	1-905449-63-1
MY TURN TO SPIN	Shaun Udal	978-1-905449-42-2
THE BEST OF ENEMIES	Kidd & McGuinness	978-1-84818-703-1
THE BODYLINE HYPOCRISY	Michael Arnold	978-1-84818-702-3
WASTED?	Paul Smith	978-1-905449-45-3

UNITED NATIONS?

AROUND THE MANCHESTER UNITED WORLD IN 80 GAMES...

Tim Webber

www.knowthescorebooks.com

First published in the United Kingdom
by Know The Score Books Ltd, 2009

Know The Score Books Limited
118 Alcester Road, Studley, Warwickshire, B80 7NT
01527 454482
info@knowthescorebooks.com
www.knowthescorebooks.com

A CIP catalogue record is available for this book from the British Library
ISBN: 978-1-84818-405-3

Jacket design by Ian Baker, Cartoon Stock

Printed by Athaeneum Press, Gateshead, Tyne & Wear UK

ACKNOWLEDGEMENTS

First and foremost I'd like to thank Clare for putting up with the whole 'adventure' and for getting me to go travelling in the first place. Hopefully it wasn't too bad! I can't thank you enough. I'd also like to thank Chris for providing a good first port of call for a few things I thought might be funny and more importantly telling me when they clearly were not (and lending me the money to go to Rome).

Thanks must also go to Simon Lowe and Know The Score for agreeing to publish the book from such an embryonic stage and the raft of varied people who either watched games with me, put me in touch with those willing to give their opinions or those who allowed the book to happen and anyone who Googled something for me when I was lost in foreign lands. There were many, here are some of you – Richard King, Tristan Edwards, James and Sarah, Ian and Alan, Rahul Bali, Neil Joshi, John Duerden, Sam Jones, Andrew Wallace, Peter Holland, Rowan Simons, Andrew Wainstein, Andy Mitten, Benjamin and Oliver Dean, Paul Kam, Jennifer Louis, Alan Graham, Emias and Hameem, Brian Torkkola, Sonny Hong, Alan Graham, David Herman, Todd Eide and the various people I chatted too without ever really knowing who you were. Thanks finally to my Mum for giving me a free place to stay while I finished writing the book having predictably returned home with no money.

Tim Webber, September 2009

Contents

Introduction

RIGHT, LET'S GET this out of the way. I am a Manchester United fan and, unfortunately as has become necessary upon revealing this to strangers, here is my defence. I went to my first United game in the 1987/88 season, aged eight, and have been going consistently since then. I am currently a season ticket holder. If you want more, then the entire side of mother's family is from Manchester (Northenden), and my Grandfather was a season ticket holder until he deemed that price increases that took the annual payment to around £12.50 were too much. At no point did I make a logical choice to support United, it just happened, it was just expected. Hopefully that covers it. If not then you're probably a Liverpool fan, in which case why have you got the book in your hands anyway? – plus if you're around my age (29) then it's you, and certainly not me, that's the 'gloryhunter'.

It's not a raw nerve as such, but given the reaction I get, particularly since moving to London for work purposes two-and-a-half years ago, it's worth establishing the situation from the off, in order to add credence to what follows.

To an extent though it's not difficult to see why United 'fans' get themselves a bad name. To me it seems completely inexplicable that someone would choose to support a team that they have no connection to whatsoever, and have no intention of going to watch on at least a semi-regular basis. An 'armchair' fan from Wiltshire or Sussex or wherever claiming that it's a 'bit far' to go to actually attend a match, or hiding consistently behind the 'you can't get tickets for Old Trafford' mantra – that has not been true for about five years – is at complete odds with what a fan (a term, of course, deriving from fanatic) should be. If it were me, I'd think, *what's the point*? How can you assume pride and joy from on-pitch events, and similarly claim to be frustrated by them (for the five to ten seconds that you are bothered), if there's no real link between you and the club?

While a lot of what I may be saying might appear harsh and a little off-putting to the casual fan, it's a context that needs setting – and believe me, is almost a moderate approach in comparison to some of the views espoused by fans who attend Old Trafford on a regular basis.

The by-product of this 'support' is that for genuine match-going Reds, like myself, there is that need to defend yourself, which for me, is the galling part. It's not just City and Liverpool fans that you need to justify yourself to, by way of idle banter, it's pretty much everyone. It's amazing how much you can immediately dislike a friend of your girlfriend's who opines upon your first meeting in a pub, when you glance up at a television to will Bolton to beat Liverpool: "Oh, why do you want Liverpool to lose so much?"

"'Cos I'm a United fan."

"Another Man U fan. I'm a Liverpool fan actually, both my boyfriend and I are."

"Really? How come?"

"No idea why he is, I only support them 'cos he tells me too. You're lucky he's not here tonight, he's gone to the cinema, but he wouldn't have liked meeting a Man U fan."

Now given that I'm not an openly rude person, it suddenly becomes necessary to excuse myself to go immediately to the toilet and mop up the blood that's about to leak out of my ear. But what I'd obviously like to have said would have been:

'Thanks for your very incisive assessment of my support of United, and I'm so glad that you felt you were able to comment on it, particularly given that you and your boyfriend are such huge Liverpool fans, what with them playing on TV tonight, and neither of you even bothering to go so far as to watch the goddamn thing!'

And that is basically what happens. That, or something pretty similar, on a fairly regular basis. And yes, as you can imagine it's pretty annoying; to myself, and I'm sure to thousands of United fans (I almost said up and down the country there).

I used to work for a sports gaming company – thus in a very football orientated environment – and a colleague summed it up pretty accurately, noting of a new employee that I'd prefer them to be a Liverpool or City fan than a 'Man U' fan. And that pretty much hits the nail on the head.

This antipathy has become such a casually referenced and prominent part of the English psyche that even those with no interest in the game, or intent to question you, take part. Two seasons ago on the way to a match at Old Trafford (I think against West Ham), two 50-something women on the train, travelling to watch Celine Dion at the MEN even got in on the act:

"Oh the train's busy."

"It's because there's a football match on. Manchester United are playing."

"Oh, right."

Clearly the end of the conversation, I hear you cry. Oh, no, not for Celine Dion fan number one. "Yeah, they travel in from all around. They say that no-one in Manchester actually supports United. They all support City."

"Oh."

Yes, that's 'oh', as in, 'I have no interest in this, nor do you, but yet you still feel the need to say it.' It's a cheap shot, and people take it. But face it, these were Celine Dion fans after all, who better placed to comment on the nature of fandom in English football?

At the ground the theme continues. A Malaysian supporters club here, ten groups of Irish fans there. It is to an extent soul destroying, the consistent dilution of what a United fan should be. In the 2007/08 season at the Munich memorial match (United lost to City), yes, the 50-year anniversary of the air disaster, my brother sat next to a young Irish lad, who was basically watching John O'Shea, Richard Dunne and Stephen Ireland. Is that a joke? Seriously. For those of you slower on the uptake, he was only interested in Irish players, and was keen to point out that "Richard Dunne's having a good game," and "Stephen Ireland's doing well." Both City players - but he was sat in a United kit. Quite simply, how does that happen? It just shouldn't be allowed to.

These 'Man U' fans ruin it for me to a degree. They do. They don't really care, they use the club as a means of improving themselves and thus shouldn't be able to share in the enjoyment of your Rooneys, Cantonas and Giggs'. The fact that they can't see that Paul Scholes is the best English player of the last ten years by a country mile, proves that they don't deserve to revel in that joy.

So, yes, I can see why United fans get a bad name. And as you can no doubt tell, it doesn't sit all that well. In fact I'd almost go as far as to say that I actively dislike these large bands of supporters, these 'day-trippers', that come and go at Old Trafford on a weekly basis – there one minute, gone the next – but perfectly willing to adopt a 'voice of the fans' attitude and tell you how you should be watching the game.

This isn't a frivolous rant, it's important to establish my personal perspective at this stage, but at the same time I'm perfectly aware of the borderline hypocrisy of what I have said. I realise that without United being commercially successful, success on the pitch in recent times would not have been so frequent. But to be honest that doesn't concern me too much, because that in essence is the beauty of being a football fan. Hypocrisy and logic don't really come into it.

On the one hand it seems perfectly natural in my mind that all the United players are great mates, and thus it's a little unsettling to find out that, for instance, Teddy Sheringham and Andy Cole never spoke, and that Roy Keane and Peter Schmeichel came to blows on the training pitch. Obviously, well logically, 20 or so people aren't all going to get on, just as in any workplace, but in my mind they do, because they all play for United.

At the same time I have a natural and instinctive dislike of all Liverpool players. Yet, this is based purely and simply around their playing for Liverpool. I've never met any of them, I don't know if I would detest them in real life. Except Jamie Carragher of course, I'd fucking hate him. Definitely.

So, it's against this backdrop that I write this book. Having watched football, and supported United all my life, and always worked in the sports/gaming environment, I'd always avoided going 'travelling' simply because I didn't want to miss any of the domestic football season. In fact the main reason I chose not to go into sports journalism was because I knew I'd rather be watching United in a League Cup tie, than something like Real against Barca. Football, or rather United, had always 'got in the way'. So travelling, during the season, had for me always been a no-go.

But, now I am going. Why? Having written this, I'm not entirely sure. But, it just seems like the right time to go, and going with the right person, certainly helps.

So, on 1 October I'm leaving England, leaving behind that most important aspect of my life: football. Perhaps that should actually read: Man United. (I'm allowed to make this statement as my girlfriend, Clare, the aforementioned 'right person' is travelling with me!)

HAVING communicated, fairly forcibly that I'm not that keen on United's world-wide fanbase, I thought it'd be very interesting to explore differences in fan culture and my own experiences of those in a unique manner. Instead of travelling 'the world' (my path of travel at this point is roughly; Russia, Mongolia, China, Vietnam, Cambodia, Japan, India, Kenya, Tanzania, South Africa, USA, home) watching a variety of local matches and drawing conclusions from them, I will write about my experience of watching United, or at least attempting to, whilst on tour. And no, this not merely an attempt to create a handy excuse to pop off around the globe and watch all United's games as I go along – that's just the cynic in you talking.

So, how will this work?

First off, this is a book about football. It is not a travel book, although given the environment in which it will be written it will examine different people in different countries. What I am mostly interested in is their knowledge of and attitudes towards football in general and United in particular, and also to find out how far the reach of the club, which claims to penetrate deep into every market, really has stretched to after years of global marketing strategy. What this book most certainly is not is a guidebook.

In order to maintain football 'purity' the fixture list will provide the recognisable structure and govern entries – this is how fans interact with the club and the players, so it seems appropriate to maintain this relationship.

It will explore fan culture through foreign fans' approach to United, thus the team will be the one constant throughout. Will I end up celebrating the worldwide nature of the fanbase or dislike it more?

It will create a unique environment that is not realistically achievable for fans in England. I will be watching United games in almost complete isolation, that is, without digesting two other Premier League games a week, and countless highlights. Also I will be without regular contact with the media. Will the conclusions that I draw from seeing games abroad be the same as those at home?

The rigid structure of the football calendar provides a core to fans' lives; will enforcing this a) impact on the experience of travelling and the supposed 'no watches, no deadlines' theory or b) will I – and I'm worried about this – find out that, despite 22 years' match-going support, I don't really care if I miss a game?

Above all, it'll be interesting to see whether it can even be done. Can you really support a team from outside the country in which they play? Can you stroll into a drinking establishment in Vietnam and get them to stick the game on? Is it possible to hold a decent debate with a Mongolian nomad on the pros and cons of Carrick and Hargreaves as a midfield partner for Scholes? There will inevitably be a few occasions when I cannot see the game, and thus come the end of the season, if United are in the hunt for honours will I feel any less involved, or less able to revel in the glory and celebration?

How will the fans I meet react to having their support questioned by me? Why did they, in the first place end up 'supporting' a club on the other side of the planet? Will they be appreciative of the fact that their support of a foreign side, instead of a team from their own league, is actually damaging the state of football in their own country? Will they recognise the absurdity of the 39th game proposal? Will they, the Americans especially, be aware of the state of the club's ownership, and will they care that United has been transformed from a financial success into a debt-ridden and extremely unstable organisation by an aggressive takeover by everyone's favourite American family, the Glazers? A takeover that has had a dramatic impact on the pockets of the match-goers who are being abused and taken for granted every time the club hikes the price of the season tickets – a 'group' of people with whom they are supposedly a part of, and thus should empathise strongly with.

From a personal point of view, how will I feel? How will it affect my own relationship with the club and English football as a whole? Will it go to dilute my passion? Will I find that I actually miss such things as the blathering of Andy Gray and his hopelessly misguided punditry?

Let's find out . . .

Russia

MOSCOW
Blackburn (a) 2-0
UK time: 4/10/08, 17.30
Local time: 4/10/08, 20.30

OK, SO I have to admit I thought this was going to be pretty easy. Clare and I had arrived in St. Petersburg a few days earlier and having noted the volume of bars, some 'English' pubs amongst them, on Nevsky Prospect, the city's main thoroughfare, I felt comfortable assuming Moscow would be similarly well equipped. You might have guessed from how this is going that it didn't quite turn out as expected.

St. Petersburg was our first stop on the entire trip and although supposedly the most westernised of cities in the former Soviet bloc, it still represented jumping in at the deep end. The dawn of a seven-month trip of unfamiliarity immediately preceded by quitting jobs and giving up our flat, aka stability, just as a worldwide financial malaise really started snow-balling was always going to produce at least momentary hesitation. Equally, it is this very freedom and impending unknown that creates antic-ipation and excitement ahead of anyone's 'epic journey', but, we'd shirked the usual advice of easing ourselves into proceedings by hitting one of the more traveller-friendly hotspots of south-east Asia or somewhere with a half-decent understanding of our mother tongue. Instead we'd ended up flying directly, via Rossiya airlines, to Russia – a country whose air safety record is the 'worst in the world' and contributed to an astonishing 42 per cent of the World's total airline fatalities in 2006.

As I sat on the plane contemplating what exactly it was that we were doing, I tried to convince myself that my feelings at this point should be entirely positive and full of the wide-eyed amazement that was to come. A timely indication of Russia's modernisation greeted me as I tore the tinfoil lid from my in-flight meal. An east meets west fusion dish lay before me – stewed beef blanketing a bed of pasta – an early pointer to the culinary delights that waited? My first bite, or rather five-minute chew, revealed I'd possibly identified the origin of those remarkably high casualty figures.

Because of the complications of landing a Russian Visa, or in our case a Russian, Mongolian and Chinese one at the same time, it had been pertinent for us to book this early portion of the trip through a specialist company to secure the letter of sponsorship necessary for the procure-ment of this documentation. Additionally there was not a single part of me that was disappointed with the upshot; namely a driver waiting for us once we made it to the arrivals hall.

'Driver' is perhaps a slightly grandiose term. A man with 'Clare' written in biro on a crumpled piece of paper and a noticeable limp seemed like our 'lift'. He signalled for us to follow him, which of course we did. I braced myself; the Hollywood moment beckoned. The moment that would instantly wash away any doubt. The moment that you step out of the arrivals hall into blazing sunshine, suffer a sensory overload as vibrant new colours wind around you; your optic nerve hums as the unfamiliar bustles by; enticing aromas swirl up your nostrils; the sound of friendly banter in foreign tongues undulates through the crisp, clear air down your external auditory meatus reverberating against your ear drum; the taste of saliva and adrenalin fills your mouth, and sweat beads penetrate the surface of your palms in anticipation. You feel energised, you're alive.

Get real, this was Russia after all. It was pissing down, it was 4.30pm and it was nearly dark. The car park was next to deserted, but strangely none of the vehicles belonged to our driver. We marched straight across it, coming to a halt outside a building site where he displayed a palms down gesture and a comedy driving motion, clearly meaning we should stay put while he shuffled off for the car.

The ten-minute soaking we endured waiting for his return was doing little to brighten the appeal of the country. Prior to leaving, a friend had kindly enlightened me with a quick and rather brutal breakdown of how I was going to die in each of the countries that we were visiting. The Russian mafia were the culprits in this part of the world, so the rather deserted nature of the building site was my paramount concern at this point. The air felt tense, this had been one of my countries of choice and I was hoping it would pull something out of the bag pretty soon to avert Clare's scorn. A car was a good start. We jumped into what was, while not exactly the old banger of Communist era propaganda, not the most salubrious ride either. The driver thrust a mobile phone towards us and some accented English spilt out of the earpiece.

On the other end of the line was Mischa, who firstly asked us if we'd been picked up by the driver, before informing us in no uncertain terms that it would take around an hour and a half to get to our hotel and that she would meet us there the following morning at 10am to take us on a three-hour walking tour of the city.

Re-invigorated, the following day St. Petersburg cut a far more welcoming place. It is amazing what a little sunlight and switching off the rain can do. Additionally Mischa seemed ready to dispel any lingering stereotypes of the forbidding place that Russia has often seemed in Western eyes. She was an articulate woman in her early twenties, fluent in English and preoccupied with her degree, which seemed to be English cultural studies of sorts and generated as many questions for us as we had for her. She was evidently a product of the 'new' Russia, one with a wider worldview than her ancestors may have, but nevertheless a portion of her character pined for an earlier regime.

Ultimately, and unfortunately, she only went to reinforce the view that, even from a purely sporting perspective, Russia is fundamentally racist. Commenting that she liked England when she was in the countryside because it was English, whereas London was "spoilt, because there are too many eastern Europeans and blacks everywhere," was naturally disap-pointing but hardly surprising considering Dick Advocaat's comments on his attempts to improve his team at Zenit St. Petersburg in May 2008.

"I would be happy to sign anyone, but the fans don't like black players. Frankly, the only players who can make Zenit stronger are dark skinned. But for us it would be impossible."

Advocaat further revealed that he would have to ask the fans' permis-sion before committing to signing a black player, and that they were unlikely to give it. Zenit are however, the only club to have such a 'policy' and at the time of writing are the only Russian top-flight club not to have any black players in their squad.

If first impressions count for a lot, then Russia wasn't doing its best to charm us. Mischa had managed to systematically denigrate England ("all the buildings are horrible and grey"), complain, ironically, about United fans in reference to the 2008 Champions League final ("we had to organise trips for Manchester and Chelsea fans, they were horrible" – fair enough, I can't imagine that would have been much fun) and tell Clare that she was, at 26, past-it ("If you were so old in Russia and not married, people would say there's something wrong with you," which naturally implied she was a lesbian). As a parting shot she left us with a stern warning. She knew that the following day we were getting the train to Moscow for our first stint on, what is incorrectly, but commonly known as, the Trans-Siberian Railway. She cautioned us against drinking even so much as a sip of alcohol in any circumstances, as her countryman would poison and steal from us, and forbade us from gambling, as the locals would cheat us out of our livelihoods. If this were all part of a negative stereotype reinforcement programme then it had succeeded.

The following night we made our way to the station. The nine-hour journey would provide a fairly light introduction to the legendary rail network, paling in comparison to the five-night, four-day adventure (Moscow to Irkukst) that we had to come. It was still an overnight trip though and we knew our level of 'enjoyment' could very much hinge on the identity of our cabin mates.

The difficulty of falling asleep on your first overnight train trip, in a tiny four berth cabin seemingly designed by an American studio boss to sum up life behind the iron curtain, cannot be underestimated. It's not just the confines of your temporary living quarters that make it unwelcoming.

Passing a passport and ticket inspection just to get on the train sets the ball rolling and involves your first meeting with your Provinista (think female character from *'Allo 'Allo* set on a Russian train), one of whom rules each coach. Our second ticket interrogation five minutes later, at the door of our cabin, elicited a scoff as it appeared our would-be roomies were a no-show, so far. We were temporarily happy, yet soon realised the peril of our ways as this only meant that every stationed stop - a halt indicated by commands blaring from loud speakers on the platform with a frighteningly metallic zeal - brought with it the fear of two Russians, doubtless out to both poison and steal from us, yanking open the door and making themselves at home.

SO, after a night bravely hidden under a blanket staring forlornly at the back of a cupboard door, dreading a seemingly inevitable arrival that never actually came, it was with little glee that I anticipated traipsing around a new city trying to find a place to watch the game that would kick-off at 8.30pm that night.

But, maybe an oracle awaited us. A note at our hotel 'informed' us that we had another three-hour walking tour scheduled for 10am, for which there was no financial compensation if we didn't turn up (some would say a clear acknowledgement that this was all too early as we had arrived at our accommodation at 6am). However, we were going, so I was sure that amongst nodding in the right places and agreeing that every-thing (including the Metro stations) was hugely impressive, and asking questions about Lenin and Stalin, I could sneak in a casual inquiry about football and where to watch it.

The guide, Danny, also seemed an excellent person to ask. Not the older more studious type, here was a student in his early twenties who lived in the centre of Moscow, a product of the 'new Russia' - ah, we've been here before. I fulfilled my role impeccably. "Yes, Moscow is much nicer than St. Petersburg." (Obviously a pressure free chance to give a real opinion.)

"How is Stalin viewed in Russia now, obviously he's not revered in the same way as Lenin, but he doesn't really get a look-in at all?" (Apparently there are now feelings that he may have been "quite bad".)

And finally: "Do you know a good bar, or have any suggestions for, where I can watch English football?"

'No idea', is a brief synopsis of Danny's response. In fact a possible shake of the head aside, it is his response in all its glory.

"Really, no suggestions?" Apparently not. It seems that no-one really cares about English football in Russia, mainly down to the strength of their domestic league and in all fairness to Danny, his assessment seems to have been correct.

With my main source of information out of the way, I knew the search was going to have to start fairly early, although I remained a little cynical about the negativity of Danny's response. The first night that we'd been in St. Petersburg, the first night of the whole trip, Russian television had opted to show the Liverpool v PSV Champions League tie, rather than a more appealing game such as Inter v Werder Bremen – an indication of interest in the Premier League I presumed. Not entirely accurately it turned out.

Danny's 'no one cares' seemed not necessarily restricted to the Premier League but also summed up many Muscovites attitude to helping foreigners in general. After identifying a bar called the Real McCoy in a *Lonely Planet* we decided to set off early, 3pm in fact, to leave plenty of time to get there, get a few beers, get into the mood, and perhaps begin the first tentative steps to challenging the reasons why people are following the club. This was the first game of our trip, and things were going to go swimmingly.

Moscow is a funny city. Beyond its centre, where the ethereal Red Square and imposing Kremlin do take the breath away, easily conjuring historic images of ruthless military might, the gloss washes away very quickly. Against this sudden change in landscape we were quite quickly going nowhere, passing sterner and sterner faces and seemingly walking towards the past. Sometimes the road names just ran out.

We decided to plough on as there wasn't much alternative if we were going to watch the game. It wasn't going swimmingly, and I felt already that I was testing Clare's patience. This was the first game, and the kick-off was only at 8.30pm; wait until we got to China and I mentioned the 2.45am kick-off. It was already evident that the boundaries of a 90-minute football match were going to sprawl unknowingly wide over the coming months.

To lighten the mood, under the rapidly dulling skies, I decided to involve her in a game of stop a Russian and get directions. After five minutes of knock-backs and plain denials of our existence, she took the honours by locating a man willing to point us down an alley seemingly in the wrong direction. But as we had nothing else to go on we trudged towards it, noticing as we did an imposing building rising up in front of us, a building I was pretty sure I recognised from the picture inlays on our map – yes, it did seem to be the ominously named 'Stalin's Apartments'.

Yep, Stalin's Apartments. Not a block of flats you'd really want to be walking around. The Roy Hattersley maisonettes are hardly comparable. I was tired, I didn't want to walk down an alley in a remote suburb of an unknown city alongside an imposing apartment building named after a man who specialised in death, or, who at the very least was 'quite bad'. But, displaying horror-film stupidity, we did it anyway.

Our first steps were not accompanied by the deep chords of a double-bass, but it did little to lift my trepidation. I'm not really sure how long the alley was but it seemed in a matter of minutes to have transported us back to the 1980s. There was a small market to the right, flanked by a couple of the obligatory Portaloos that are ten-a-penny in Moscow, and while the market wasn't deserted it also didn't have that inherent joie de vivre that one might naturally associate with a trading hub. Instead this seemed to be a bleaker Russia, the sort that you'd imagine of old, with queues for bread under freezing skies. The sun had certainly disappeared, perhaps blocked entirely by the building (but I think just covered by clouds), contriving to produce the most unwelcoming of scenarios and I have to admit I did just consider turning back immediately. Any illusions that I'd retained that we could blend in and not look touristy were quickly out the window; it was pretty evident this wasn't a place for the likes of us.

We began to make our way around the apartments as that seemed to be where the pub should be. The 'cold-war' illusion was shattered a little by an imposing Nike advert strewn across a building nearby, but this didn't seem a likely venue for a pub that would be showing Premier League matches, and certainly didn't look to be at all au fait with Sky Sports' manicured image of the English game. The back of the flats only seemed to lead to a more residential area that was pretty devoid of anything apart from old bricks and uneven pavement. But this was where the bar was supposed to be. There was a public building, but it certainly wasn't the Real McCoy, a pub in my mind I'd imagined to be blue, almost like a pack of Salt 'n' Vinegar McCoys. Instead this structure had an orange facade, and was called . . . something in Russian. A few uninterrupted minutes debating whether to go in or not were more than possible given the desertion. This couldn't be it though. We walked around some more, heading momentarily towards the zoo, but a couple of minutes later, with the sky darker, we were back in front of a certain tangerine temple called . . . something in Russian.

Having decided this was it, or must have *been* it, and having seen a couple of 'studenty' looking people come out, we decided to go in. It wasn't it. Although it might once have been as it was set up for sport. A giant screen at one end encouraged for a while, and a couple of ridiculously-sized beers made the place more relaxing, but it was Danny's assessment in microcosm. A Dinamo Moscow game began and we soon located a menu of sorts detailing, in Russian (and thus Cyrillic script) the day's viewing schedule. Deduction enabled us to surmise that it was back to back Russian football for the day ahead and thus there was to be no fruit borne here.

It's times like this when you wish you could just ask someone, but our attempts proved that the language barrier was still pretty significant in that part of town. So, where next? We had another beer to gather our thoughts and having exhausted the information in our guidebook, that had of course led us there in the first place, it was time to call for some help.

I thought about a couple of people at home who I knew had nothing better to do than to sit at a computer, or in the vicinity of one, on a Saturday afternoon and sent them some text messages while I finished my drink. Within minutes, they both came back to me. An American sportsbar named 'Willow' was a possibility on 'the strip' and failing that there was an Irish pub in the same vicinity. We had addresses with road numbers and everything.

Yes thank you. This all sounded promising. Ignoring my earlier attempts to blend in and keep my glances at a map a furtive secret, the whole thing was unfolded on the table. The bars were pin-pointed and we were ready to roll. It was like we'd suddenly found a way to blend in with the 80s nostalgia and were about to run out of the pub, flanked by Anneka Rice, and jump into a helicopter. But alas not. We were out of the building though, back past the market, down the alley, each step taking us back to the future: 1983, 84, 85… and to be perfectly honest the place was just not that scary anymore as looking at the map had revealed that the building wasn't even Stalin's apartments anyway - they were on the other side of town.

So, to the strip. The bloody strip. The longest road in the world it seemed. And we started at the wrong end. We got to the top eventually but the Irish pub was closed and the American sportsbar was now a Japanese restaurant. This was all too hard, I was far too tired. This wasn't the way it was meant to be. We had nowhere to look and there was only half an hour until kick-off. With the final hope that the hotel would be able to show the match (they couldn't), as they had a Chelsea flag in the bar (apparently a gesture of solidarity with some dismayed fans staying there in May 2008), we trudged back to the Metro to begin the 30-minute journey back to base. Exiting the underground system we took a wrong turn, deciding to retrace our steps just in time as a bottle shattered on the floor ten feet behind us.

I sent another text message, a message of failure, to my brother asking him to keep me up to date with any goals. The two that we did score, in a match we have often laboured in brought some glee, although the over-riding feeling was disappointment. It was the first game, and I hadn't managed to watch it in what was supposed to be a fairly westernised country, in a not overly prohibitive timezone. Not exactly how I'd seen things going. 'Our easiest win there for a while,' was how my brother summed the game up, and it was annoying to have tried so hard yet not be able to take much joy from the goals. The single message that I took from the experience was to do some research ahead of time, but a part of me was regretting the trip at all. If it was going to continue like this then I didn't have all that much enthusiasm for it. Watching United was obviously not going to be as simple as I'd hoped.

Russia, in summary, is not the best place to watch English football. They are, to paraphrase Danny, 'not interested'. They have their own league, and that's all they really care about, and to be honest, why not? They are proud to have a product that is growing in strength and increasing their sense of identity in a global sport. It's easy to forget that in many ways Russia is a new country, as new as many of the other former members of the Soviet Union, particularly in its relationship with other nations, and football, and sport in general will be a defining factor in shaping that development. This is not just frivolous comment – I witnessed to a degree the depth of nationalism it inspires a couple of days later.

On the five-day train journey from Moscow to Irkutsk, our train cabin was filled for one night by a businessman, who spoke a very small amount of English. After an hour of broken conversation had revealed the information that he worked in timber, was in fact from Minsk in Belarus, was travelling to Irkutsk for business and had been on holiday to Sweden a lot as one of his clients lived there and they spoke the language of whisky, there was a five-minute lapse. Seemingly the limits of polite conversation had been reached, when suddenly the man hit upon something: "Manchester?" he bellowed, almost surprising himself.

"Yes."

"Football?"

"Yes, Manchester United, I support them."

"Ha, Zenit, Zenit, Zenit!"

"Ah, the Super Cup . . ." (which United had half-heartedly lost a month earlier.)

"Zenit, Zenit," this time accompanied by some international sign language, for 'up-yours'. This went on for about five minutes. A middle-aged businessman, who wasn't even Russian, telling me how happy he was, or more like how shafted I'd been by Zenit. It was only stopped by me showing him a picture of the Zenit team in *World Soccer*, before he finished with a last triumphant "Zenit!", and soon after went to bed.

China

BEIJING

West Brom (h) 4-0
UK time: 18/10/08, 17.30
Local time: 19/10/08, 00.30

Celtic (h) 3-0
UK time: 21/10/08, 19.45
Local time: 22/10/08, 02.45

AFTER THE MOSCOW disappointment (an unlikely phrase to hear in a United context following our Champions League triumph in the city) an international break followed for which I was actually grateful for once. Usually heralding a two-week barren spell where club games are replaced by an innate obligation to watch a slightly floundering England team prove that the Premier League is hugely indebted to its foreign imports by playing the 'Liverpool way', on this occasion it afforded us time to travel through Siberia and Mongolia where I wouldn't have been hugely optimistic of getting access to the games. Confidence was a little low after the debacle of the Blackburn game, and the fortnight's break was a great chance to prove to Clare that chasing United across the globe wasn't going to consume our trip.

By the time of the next match, a home game against West Brom, we were in China, and I'd been doing my research since Moscow. A tip-off from Beijing based author Rowan Simons had identified three potential venues; the Den, Frank's Place and Paddy O'Shea's. The recent closure of the Club Football Centre had apparently robbed the capital of any genuine 'Chinese' places to watch Premier League games, another untimely closure for a certain guidebook's publication cycle. Having checked them out on the internet in the Ulaanbaatar post office (which aside from the opportunity to send postcards from Outer Mongolia offered easily the fastest internet connection in Asia, but with very small chairs) and procured addresses for them all, Frank's Place was the chosen recipient of our custom, mainly because it had a schedule on the site that confirmed the game would be shown.

Our arrival into the city was again on match day via an overnight train, a two-day trip in fact from Ulaanbaatar. The Chinese trains are very similar to their Russian counterparts, perhaps slightly more modern, and with the delightful addition of a 7am wake-up call courtesy of the guards' morning phlegming session, which lasts approximately half an hour. Hoik five times, spit, and repeat. Sleep had again been thin on the ground, with a four-hour border stop at midnight, involving cabin inspections and requiring us to stay awake for the duration. As the spit hit the pan and I decided not to continue dreaming of mucus, I lay there and began reflecting on the relationship between United and China.

There was of course a history here; the club toured the country as part of their Asian tours in 1999, 2005 and 2007 and returned again in summer, 2009. It was in fact the only country they were choosing to visit on all three of their most recent trips. They had launched two Chinese versions of their own website, one in traditional and one in simplified Chinese, in July 2005 extending the penetration of the Pravda-esque communication arm of which the Chinese Communist party would have been proud . . . and spit.

IF we are to believe the hype, then United have 20 million fans in just China alone (although as usual take with the required tub of salt) which coupled with dramatic economic growth make it the obvious target for the club. While there may be many that are interested in the club can they truly be classed as fans? Of course not. The 2007 tour match wasn't even a sell-out, and sales for the 2009 game were particularly slow in China before eventually hitting a reported maximum allowance, someway below capacity. The problem of loyalty remains and, as Rowan Simons indicates in his book *Bamboo Goalposts*, it's common for fans to follow a number of top European teams at once, and match allegiances with the undulations of success. With no generational effect there is no reason, aside from the tours (according to a 2005 Birkbeck University study, seeing the players in the flesh is vital) and the stockpiling of trophies to follow the team, thus any commercial activity can surely only have a fleeting impact in the face of such fickleness? While Budweiser lighting up pitchside messages in Mandarin characters might make sense, United aren't a comparable commodity and just can't function in the same way . . . and spit.

This spitting 'thing' was interesting. Clare had visited Beijing previously and had regaled me with a tale of an elderly lady removing her face mask and landing a ball of phlegm an inch from the end of her foot. I'd naturally taken it to be Clare's fault and dismissed it, but as an Englishman primarily interested in football, I was well versed in the theory that spitting at someone was the epitome of unsportsmanlike behaviour, and was finding it a little off-putting to say the least. However, it wasn't until that evening, sitting in a restaurant when a 'gentleman' at the table next to us paused between mouthfuls to spit directly onto the floor between our tables, that I actually recoiled with the sort of horror that my parents routinely hammed up when footballers spitting on the television seemed endemic in the late 80s, early 90s.

Perhaps though this was a key link between the Chinese and United; the driving force behind their popularity. Throughout the early Premier League years was the United teamsheet, or subs list at least, not routinely adorned with the name of Brian McClair? The Scottish forward-cum-midfielder was not only famous for being the original squad player, the only footballer of his time capable of irony and a footballer whose sexuality wasn't called into question just because he read a broadsheet, but he was also uniquely skilled in the expulsion of unwanted spittle. Where kids across the world may have attempted to mimic a spectacular Mark Hughes volley or Ryan Giggs' snake-hipped dribbling, there were nearly as many who would attempt to shoot mucus from their nostrils without making a mess of their shirts. McClair was the undoubted master of this, even capable of running and snotting all in one movement.

In fact, could China's love-affair with David Beckham not be similarly traced? The seminal moment of the midfielder's early career was of course his goal, scored from inside his own half, against Wimbledon. It announced him to the world. In celebration Beckham raised both his hands in the air, turned, and right in front of the camera gobbed out one of the biggest balls of spit you're every likely to see. And, who was the first team-mate to reach the future star? Yes, McClair himself: 'Great expectoration son. Nice goal too.' Beckham had arrived. Disappointingly for the Chinese audience, Beckham's flob appears to have been edited from most highlights reels that are shown these days, but still I thought I was onto something.

We carefully left the restaurant at about 10pm and jumped into a cab. I'd been told that Beijing closing times operated on a 'if you're in here we'll serve you' basis, so was keen to get there pretty early to ensure that nothing stupid like a closed pub was going to get in the way of the game. We were also due to meet a couple of other United fans that we'd met in a Ger Camp in Mongolia (cue cheap jokes), so a few drinks beforehand would be more than agreeable. At least that's how I was selling it to Clare.

Although we had a map with road names printed in Roman and Chinese characters, communicating with the taxi driver was problematic as we were looking for an address that basically amounted to 'near the Rosedale Hotel'. Our initial conversations with him didn't seem to be going all that well. I'd point at the hotel on the map, he'd look confused, so I'd point at it again as though my initial point had perhaps been a little haphazard or sloppy and that a second attempt would lead to a clear understanding. Of course it made no real difference, so I tried saying the name of the hotel and pointing at the same time. The result was a slight understanding, a momentary breakthrough, before outright confusion again. Eventually pointing did seem to work, but not in a simple 'look at the end of my finger, that's the hotel we'd like to go to' way, but in a 'this is where we are now, we want to go in this direction towards this hotel' kind of a way. It was a more complicated style of pointing, and it seemed I was good at it. He had it.

The journey started pleasantly enough, but ten minutes in we hit a dual carriageway that appeared to be heading out of the city – a little strange given my belief that Frank's Place was indeed a place within the city centre, off-centre perhaps but not a real road away. *Relax, I told myself, this is fine, the taxi driver knows the way, it's probably a traffic dodging method, no doubt it just cuts out a big chunk of the crowded roads.* This logic didn't really add up given it was after 10pm, and while the roads were still busy, they weren't exactly prohibitive to driving.

I stole a couple of glances at Clare, and her half smile told me she was thinking the same, namely: *where the hell are we? And where the hell are we going?* but without a similar concern over missing the football. The meter was mercifully low as I calculated the cost of a return fare, so I smiled back, the face of confident reassurance, and took my map out again. We'd been in the taxi for about 25 minutes now and I was wondering whether another bout of pointing was necessary.

After about 35 minutes I was 95 per cent sure that this now qualified as a kidnapping, but not wanting to cause a fuss I sat back and kept my mouth shut. At 45 minutes I voiced my concern half-jokingly: "Are we being kidnapped?" (This to Clare, not a polite inquiry to the driver-cum-ransom demander.)

"Ha."

"Seriously."

"You wanted to try and walk there!"

"Yes I know. But what should we do now? It can't be this far."

"Hold on." We were pulling off the dual carriageway and promisingly there were a few hotels around, one of which was the Rosedale. Once out of the car we amazingly selected the correct direction and within three minutes were sitting at a table in Frank's Place and I was choosing which of the 3 o'clock kick-offs (of which they were showing two) to focus on.

Relief swept over me. A combination of the Russian experience and more sleep deprivation had made me feel like we'd never get there, but I was actually in a position in Beijing where I was going to be able to watch Manchester United play football. So what that it was just on television, in an ex-pat bar that was empty by kick-off? It had been hard travelling so far and the 18 days since leaving the UK had felt much, much longer, and thus an unfeasibly big, chasm-like gap since I last watched a game. The other two we were waiting for turned up soon after, with an almost identical story of a painfully long taxi drive, which for them had taken in a side trip to a sports stadium. But it just didn't seem to matter all that much anymore.

Clare commented that it was the first time I'd smiled all day, which she seemed to find disappointing. The game itself was the kind of routine success fans crave – a 4-0 win over West Brom was perfectly satisfactory. There was little to be learnt from the game in relation to United's season, or the club's presence in China, but the chance to watch the game was good enough. It was the first home game since I'd been away, and thus the first time I was definitely missing the match-day experience. It felt strange not being there, sharing in the enjoyment.

At the final whistle, the four of us – and the two other remaining customers – left the bar and got into taxis. Our final task was trying to get into our accommodation; as we were to experience quite often on returning late throughout the trip, a lot of cheap digs don't have 24-hour access and the ability to climb a gate or fence became a much used skill. By 3.30am we were in bed asleep, and I at least was happy, not dwelling on how much effort it had taken to watch a game against West Brom.

The next game came along just three days later and presented a pretty uninviting 2.45am kick-off. If that wasn't enough to make you feel tired, then a scheduled finish time of 4.30am should do the job. This time I chose Paddy O'Shea's, hoping to cut down on the return travel time, maybe meaning we could be asleep by as early as 5.30am. I know, I felt lazy. The obvious question was: how could you keep this up on a regular basis?

Would a change of venue really bring a change of luck; would it be that simple? I questioned Paul Kam, the chairman of Pro Events who have dealt with United's biannual tours since 1995 (2003 was skipped in favour of the US), to try and get a different appreciation of United's objectives. As expected he played a straight bat with most lines of enquiry, failing to stray beyond the club's objective to be the number one team in the region. He did however express the belief that the club was using the tour in part to 'thank' the fans for their support (something match-goers would probably appreciate), and that the consistency of their visits was the only way to achieve long-term success. What was most revealing however were his answers relating not so closely to football itself but to the difference in culture, and he continually returned to the adage, 'people like to be associated with success.' When I pushed along these lines, to establish that in fact real football support has nothing to do with success, being far more tribal in origin, and that 'gloryhunting' is frowned upon in England, he still could not see the problem, drawing parallels with car ownership. There was a cultural divide that on the one hand made my questions seem strange to him, and his answers similarly so to me. Are United supporters in China 'gloryhunters'? Yes, they bloody well are, but to grasp why, it's necessary to understand the principle of 'face' in their culture and how their own internal football failures make them ripe for United.

Our western faces were doing a good job of reminding us how different things can still be even though 'the world is a small place'. It had started with a trip to the Great Wall when a Chinese man had pointed at me and then at his camera, handed it to Clare and stood proudly alongside me to have his picture taken and had peaked when I was trying to take a photo of Clare on some steps in a park and an elderly lady from a Chinese tour group was brave enough to sit by her to have her picture taken as well. It opened the floodgates as the 20 or so women swirled around her, taking it in turns to be snapped alongside the strange-looking English girl. I got bored waiting and went to sit on a bench.

It was surprising. I'd obviously heard about these impromptu photo ops occurring; but in Beijing that had so recently suffered the foreign onslaught of the Olympic games? There were plenty of these small nuggets of difference – being able to choose from a 'tasty' seahorse on a stick or McDonald's from either side of the main shopping square – illustrating that attempts to assimilate the west into the east was very much an ongoing process. So perhaps China, or not everyone in it, was yet fully ready to embrace the Premier League and all it entailed. And even those that were, were still distinctly Chinese enough only to associate themselves with a big team: Manchester United.

We arrived at the pub at 11pm, with three-and-a-half-hours remaining until kick-off. I went to the bar and ordered some drinks, noticing that our stay was not going to be as long as that of a Celtic fan and his partner who were already in position. This wasn't purely an intuitive assessment of a man from a distance. I'm not able to just look at someone and immediately identify his football allegiance, he was simply wearing a Celtic shirt.

"ARE they showing the game?" I asked as I walked past the table.

"They're not sure," he replied in an Irish accent (what else?).

"They're not sure?" I reiterated, a little confused as he was surely here to watch the game. It couldn't be coincidental that a man in a Celtic shirt was sat in a sports bar in Beijing on a Tuesday night if he had no intention of watching a match they were about to play in.

"They said they might if there was interest, but they can't be sure."

"Right."

"There's somewhere else called Le Lens, that might have it."

"You mean the Den?" I countered with the smug satisfaction of someone who'd done his pub research and wasn't going to sit around in the forlorn hope that when it got to 3am that they didn't just kick everyone out. "Thanks."

I enquired at the bar and the response was affirmative; if we were still there then they would show it. So now it was merely a case of wasting three-and-a-half hours. Alcohol helped pass the time, as did locating a pool table and darts board upstairs, but it was quite hard work, and this was merely to get to the kick-off and not the match itself. Soon after we'd made our way upstairs the Celtic fan and his partner followed and then spent the next two or so hours circling us. Where we had played pool, he played pool, where we'd thrown darts he was taking over. Within 15 minutes of returning downstairs, about 40 minutes prior to kick-off, he was there too. It seemed that my ability to replicate the phonetic utterance 'the Den' had made me a kind of football oracle for him; he was clearly hanging on my every move.

When the magical moment finally arrived, there were three people at the bar occupied by a combination of the United and Arsenal matches, plus myself, Clare and the Celtic couple. The last remaining natives had stumbled out 20 minutes before. I was pleased to have made it to kick-off. It was like a perverse endurance reality TV show where people had to prove their fandom by outlasting other supporters to watch games at the stupidest time of night. I felt we were in with a strong chance of winning. We after all were not afraid to say things to people's faces, a vital component in any TV hopeful's armoury. To think of all those who had failed down the years by directing comments at an elbow or a stray knee-cap.

ESPN stream Sky Sports' Champions League coverage and thus there was the familiar 'Battle of Britain' well, crap, before the game. Would Celtic be able to show they are as good as the English Champions? How would they fare in the Premier League? No and not very well were my two guesses. Turns out I was right.

The Celtic fan however, had obviously been hoping for something quite different. Bemoaning every decision, and every goal, he whined his way through the game. But still, what did he really expect? At 2-0 his misplaced anger was growing all the time, and doing an excellent job of reminding me why I don't like watching football in pubs in the first place; it was like having an ITV commentator sat directly behind me. However, it was now 4am and so I should surely have been feeling a slight bit of camaraderie? After all he was there. Although not for much longer.

At 4.15am, 3-0 down and with only 15 minutes left it was time for him to go. At 2-0 he must have thought it was a dead cert that a player with a plain Scottish name was going to do something miraculous and get the Bhoys back in it. Just two of us remained watching United. Clare for some reason had taken a liking to the Juventus v Real Madrid game, which was strange given that at a rough guess she could have identified Ruud van Nistelrooy and little else.

The other interested party was the owner himself, and without the option of asking a native about the popularity of the club, I thought I'd ask him. I guess predictably in a place named Paddy O'Shea's he too turned out to be Irish, and was a United 'fan'. I decided to let that slide given I could have stood outside the megastore on a Saturday to follow that line of questioning. Instead I asked him about the lack of fans watching this game. His answers were much as expected. The time of the match was the main reason, but in general there was a lack of interest in the early stages of the Champions League in China, and that for the final itself it'd been packed. Predictably what I would have thought.

The time was clearly a factor, and I was feeling that myself. But that only went to further my complete lack of understanding as to why anyone would choose to support a club so far out of their own time-zone in the first place. At full-time, we dragged ourselves off our seats with about as much finesse as the pub's namesake, John, and staggered to a taxi. This wasn't what watching football was about. This was hardly enjoyable.

A long lie-in was required to recover after getting to bed just after 5am. The obvious constant in watching United, or trying to watch

United, so far was tiredness. It clearly ate into the following day as well, which for us meant that we weren't really up for much sight-seeing. An evening trip to the Beijing Olympic Park was hugely rejuvenating though and even two months after the closing ceremony it was an amazingly invigorating place to visit. The startlingly proximity of the Birds Nest Stadium to the Watercube needs to be seen to be believed and only goes to strengthen the life-affirming spirit that still emanates from every corner. It certainly wasn't difficult to imagine a vibrant atmosphere shooting through every vein of the park, bringing the surroundings to life, as Usain Bolt blasted his way into the world's consciousness in August 2008.

However, there was the nagging thought that this was all a little 'plastic' and wasn't real China at all. Reports the previous summer of the employment of 'cloud seeding' and the closing of factories nearby to try to control the weather and stem pollution during the games all made me wonder was this Olympic Park, and the success of the games themselves, a false representation? Sport as a political tool, as a form of nation building, is hardly new but was it more extreme in Beijing, and in fact didn't the country's relationship with football and the likes of Manchester United sit completely at odds with this ethos?

The Olympics were without doubt a multi-faceted show of strength from the Chinese, but it just so happened that in the world's biggest sport of all, football, it was another customary display of weakness. The high point for China in the international game came with qualification for the 2002 World Cup, a false dawn only achieved because Asian powerhouses Japan and South Korea booked their tickets as hosts and one that ended disastrously with three defeats and no goals for. Together with a multitude of domestic failings the country now seems resigned to importing football as a commodity, and the Birds Nest ironically played a culpable part in this when it hosted the Italian Super Cup in August 2009.

But will China not become too draining a market for a single club? The NBA is becoming successful in financial terms in China because it is marketing itself as a competition. Football lives and dies by its rivalries and the 'banter' between fans – the club cannot exist in isolation in a time-zone that means it's difficult for fans to get together to discuss football or pass their own interests to others (a number of Red Cafés were set-up but have all since closed). Ultimately it will be too time absorbing to secure a permanent fan base. In light of such, Premier League teams that are playing fellow Premier League teams in pre-season tournaments in Asia seem to be closer to the mark, and by extrapolation means the implausible 39th game proposition would have more long-term benefit.

The NBA does of course have its trump-card in Yao Ming, the basketball star who carried China's flag at the Olympics. United's own Ming, Dong Fangzhuo, may have been released eventually, but the club's persistence with the player was surely an attempt to exploit Chinese patriotism to build a lasting bridge between Old Trafford and Beijing. His debut in a 'real' fixture had come towards the end of the 2006/07 season at Stamford Bridge with the title already wrapped up. Anyone who was there to see it cannot have gone away with even the slightest hope for his future at the club. Young players have of course in the past had inauspicious debuts that have disappointed, but attacking players in particular usually have a surety of touch and a basic level of technical ability, or an outstanding attribute that justifies them being on the books. Dong had none of that. His lack of simple ball control was what had struck me most, it was as though he spent the entire game checking to make sure his feet were still where they should be. It remains, in the eyes of many United fans, the starkest example of United's desire for global conquest infringing on the team.

The club, of course, and Sir Alex Ferguson, disappointingly, paid lip-service to the talent he had; Fergie said he had a "big chance". Simply not true. When questioned along these lines it was significant that Paul Kam dodged the issue as best he could: "This is a question to be answered more appropriately by the Club and not me. Even though I know the answer to it, I don't think I should answer it." We all do Paul, we all do.

Vietnam

HANOI

Everton (a) 1-1
UK time: 25/10/08, 12.00 noon
Local time: 25/10/08, 18.00

AMERICAN CINEMA'S ONE-TIME obsession with the lush landscape of Vietnam has left an indelible mark on the Western mind. As such luminaries as Francis Ford Coppola and Oliver Stone sought to capture the horrors of an ill-conceived conflict, they succeeded in painting a highly intriguing picture of a country that has become the byword for east-Asian exoticism sitting high-up on many traveller's itineraries.

Such cinematography was not entirely apt for us as we were arriving in the north to the capital Hanoi, while most of the 'Vietnam conflict' (if you believe the Americans) or the 'Vietnam aggression war' (if you believe the Vietnamese), took place in the south. However, the sub-tropical land-scape that greets you as you chug across the border by train from China is still the epitome of those celluloid images, only going to whet the appetite in anticipation.

We appeared to be developing a knack of arriving in new places in the early hours of a match day after an overnight train journey, and so once again our first impressions were to be dictated by the search for football. The game in question was an away trip to Everton – normally an entertaining affair and certainly more highly anticipated than the previous three matches. Following the success of being able to watch the games in Beijing (I was clearly setting a low-bar to denote such an event a success), I had adopted a similar approach of pre-match research to locate a potential venue.

Hanoi may be a backpacker hotspot, catering to the travellers' needs and desires, or succinctly, but unromantically, as one of our travelling companions summarised: "It's easy. Everyone who needs to speak English, speaks English," but I'd only come up with one place; the Spotted Cow. Luckily, Clare and I are both of the opinion that the best way to get to know a new place is simply to walk around as much as possible. So after a quick shower and some food we set off early to explore with our only real goal being a bit of bar reconnaissance ahead of the game. We were an hour closer to home now, but the 12pm UK kick-off was still, at 6pm, five-and-a-half hours away.

Perhaps a further indictment of the Premier League's influence abroad was the Spotted Cow being more the lesser-Spotted Cow and proving particularly elusive. As the analogy doesn't stretch any further, and you can't really catch a glimpse of a building as it runs through the under-growth, you'd be right in thinking that it didn't appear anywhere as we walked the length and breadth of Pho Hai Ba Trung, the road it should have inhabited. Obviously the address should have helped, but when you can't guarantee that the buildings are ordered sequentially, in a sensible fashion, you end up scouring a whole area.

As scorching sun belted down on our backs for the first time on the trip, we again seemed to be walking around fairly aimlessly. The sheer volume of mopeds on the roads of Hanoi is a sight to behold in itself, and one poorly conceived road crossing can cost you about five minutes and a vastly increased adrenal flow as you attempt to reverse the mistake. It's like playing a human game of Frogger, in which instead of a log on which to jump to avoid the oncoming onslaught, you just have another moped. It was in these conditions that I came to realise that I didn't react that well to these aimless hunts, high temperatures and people trying to sell me a photocopied guidebook for double its UK cover price. I was quickly getting irritated by the whole thing, and was perfectly happy to blame the internet for a lack of up-to-date information.

In the vicinity of where the Spotted Cow should have been sited, there was an American Embassy Bar, and so I thought it worth enquiring as to the whereabouts of the haunt we were searching for, or indeed if it even existed. So in Clare went. After passing a giant inflatable witch on the way in, a part of their Halloween celebrations that night – which I deemed an unwelcome distraction – a woman inside directed us down the road to a place named Joe Joe 3, which had once been the Spotted Cow. So with a photo of Clare and a giant inflatable witch in the bag, we headed back in the other direction, because if we are going to waste our time looking for places to watch football, then we could also stop to take photos of giant inflatables, ok?

A quick look around Joe Joe 3, a small restaurant, revealed the lack of both a television and a desire to show the game. The owner came out to greet her only customers, but unfortunately we weren't sticking around. We managed to explain to her that we were looking for football, or at least sport of some sort and wanted to watch it on a big television screen. She told us there was a place called 'Jaspas' or 'Jaspers' that was off in the direction that we had come, mentioning that the Hanoi Towers were close. In fact what happened was that she asked us if we knew the Hanoi Towers and of course I said yes.

We headed back in the direction we had come. "Right, so do you know which way we're going?" I queried ten or so metres down the road.

"No. Towards the Hanoi Towers though."

"Yeah, where are they?"

"Don't you know?"

"No."

"So why did you say yes when she said the Hanoi Towers?"

"Well, cos, you know . . . it was easier," I confessed, realising that logic wasn't wholly on my side. This was early evidence of a theme emerging, namely my inability to ask anything properly. I am by nature quite shy, so at every possible opportunity would either send Clare to ask for me if she was willing (which thankfully with gentle persuasion was about 80 per cent of the time) or as on this occasion would blindly agree to anything I was told to bring the encounter to an end as quickly as possible, whether or not I knew what the other person was talking about, or even understood the words that they were using.

"So where are we going?" Clare asked.

"Well, she pointed in this direction, so it must be here somewhere. Come on," I called back as we began passing the same restaurants and bars (we stopped at one that had a television, to enquire. It was a flat 'no'. No, he wasn't going to speak to us. I had to ask at this one given Clare's flat refusal, punishment for my Hanoi Towers agreement), and the ridiculously large number of electrical outlets on Pho Hai Ba Trung – all swelling way beyond their capacity and surely over-estimating the need of the average Vietnamese family for a flat screen TV. The Hanoi Tower or Towers perhaps weren't coming into view, and as televisions overtook washing machines on a two to one basis, and electrical outlets of any sort overtook any other shops by a similar ratio, it dawned on me that in the same way that I was agreeing with what the restaurant manager was saying to me while being very unsure of its message, she too was probably puzzled by what the two English people standing in the doorway of a restaurant with no intention of buying any food were on about, and that maybe, just maybe, she thought we wanted to buy a television, and that was why she had directed us down Hanoi's own Silicon Alley. The heat aside, this whole escapade was beginning to have a Russian feel to it – the walking, the not-finding, the non-existence of bars that were supposed to be there. It was another slog. All I wanted to do was watch the goddamn football.

The Hanoi Tower did appear, and Jaspas, as it turned out to be, was a strange kind of American themed bar-cum-restaurant in the middle of an expensive looking hotel. While they agreed to show the game later that evening, the drink prices weren't in keeping with the general theme of Vietnamese life so I took the bold step of labelling this our 'back-up' choice, a little like naming substitutes without having a starting XI.

I was however, probably a little groundlessly, confident of finding somewhere else if we just returned to the 'French Quarter', the area of the city most frequently trodden by travellers and tourists. Winding streets, sunglasses and flip-flop sellers, bag pushers, proprietors of 'authentic' local arts – this place had everything you could want from a cheap Spanish resort, aside from a hen party and a stuffed donkey. It certainly wasn't the

Vietnam that I'd expected, or wanted. The sporadic moped sticker of a United crest and a couple of football shirt sightings had raised my interest though. It was the first sign of the club that I'd seen on the trip as both Russia and China had been devoid of any United symbolism, outside of the two sports bars where we'd watched matches. Surely this constituted evidence of local interest, and thus more avenues for watching the game?

When greeted with what amounts to a cobbled Curly Wurly, it's hard to know which path to take, and the absence of a destination can almost be your worst enemy. Any signs of hesitation are taken by your closest street vendor to suggest that you are ripe for business, and the cardinal sin of stopping elicits a familiar exchange:

"Hello."

"No thanks."

"You want to buy a book? Very good books."

"No thanks."

And that should really be it. But Clare has patience that can almost not be tried. So whilst I would throw in a cursory 'no thanks', or in a lot of cases merely ignore the approach, she, possibly I think to prove to me that 'you can say no, and still be nice', but more likely for the direct purpose of pissing me off, would entertain the questioner. Especially when she knew that the conversation might go like this:

Street Vendor: "Hello."

Me: "No thanks."

Clare: "No thanks."

SV: "You want to buy a book? Very good books."

C: "Not at the moment thanks."

SV: "Cheap price."

Me: "No."

C: "Maybe later."

Me: "Don't say later he'll wait for us."

SV: "Yes later."

Me: "See?"

SV: "Where are you from?"

Me: "Bye."

C: "England."

SV: "Ah, London?"

C: "No not really."

SV: "Manchester?"

C: "Sort of."

SV: "Ah Manchester, very good football."

C: "Yes, he supports them."

SV: "Ah sir, Wayne Rooney, Wayne Rooney."

Me : "So do you support them?"

SV: "Huh?"

Me: "Manchester United?"

SV: "Yes, very cheap price. Very good book."

And her goal was reached. While she stopped short of saying, 'Huh, another one,' I'm pretty sure that she was tallying the number of people she could get to say 'Wayne Rooney, Wayne Rooney' to me in the space of a day. I was getting more agitated, but strangely Clare was nonplussed. It seemed she had come to terms with the day being written off so it didn't really matter how long it took to find a place to watch it. She knew we were meeting another couple (James and Sarah) for a few drinks at five, and whether or not that bar had the football really made no difference.

Yet again I was tired. The heat and humidity were rising, the number of people bustling by was increasing and the volume and noise of the traffic growing, all making Hanoi seem hugely claustrophobic and exacerbating its unfamiliarity. These conditions routinely leave you paralysed with indecision and ten minutes glaring at shelves of mineral water just in case you make a gross miscalculation and choose the wrong brand ultimately costing you about thirteen pence more is not uncommon. I felt I was plummeting towards that low-ebb and seeking to exploit that to the max an evil genius watching from the underworld obviously signalled: 'Roll out the fat kid!'

Here he came. Riding towards us on a bicycle. Protected somehow. Occupying a segment of the road that no moped could touch, and that no pedestrian could hope to reach. In a perverse spin on the red dressed young girl that dominates the black and white landscape of *Schindler's List* the portly little scamp was also wearing red, but this time it was a United shirt. All I could think as he sailed past us was, *I bet he knows where to watch the game.*

We had to get a semblance of control. Could we go back to Jaspas for the game? Possibly. But James and Sarah weren't hugely interested in the match and I felt it was a good opportunity to combine the football with a night out and thus lessen the drain on time that it was probably becoming to Clare.

I found a slightly quieter corner of the street to look in our guidebook, and while there were no direct mentions of football, there were a couple of places highlighted for being popular with 'ex-pats'. Le Pub took my eye, potentially because of the subtle intelligence of its naming. A bar in a French Quarter, named Le Pub, clever. For those struggling with the most rudimentary French, in this case the word 'Le' means 'the', while the icing on the cake (or croissant) is clearly that the word 'pub' means 'pub'.

Predictably, it was in the opposite direction. As we rounded the first corner we were greeted with the sight of the rotund child in a United shirt, riding his bike down the centre of one of the planet's most dangerous roads without a care in the world. He was taunting us, or rather me, and I'm sure he was enjoying every minute of it. I tell you if I'd had a doughnut I'd have stamped on it right in front of his massive face.

We ploughed on trying to keep the faith, and about 20 minutes later Le Pub stood before us. We went inside for a drink, and spotted a television in the corner. I asked the obvious question. It caused momentary confusion about the kick-off time but they soon agreed to show it later that evening, which in retrospect was generous given the sign on the wall that said 'Premier League football shown here every Saturday'. This certainly seemed a better option for watching the game with the sheer number of locals in the vicinity surely guaranteeing some local 'support'.

After a quick drink at about a third of the price of Jaspas, we left, passing a fat cycling child on the way. With a venue secured my bubbling resentment had subsided somewhat, and I did begin to wonder, *with all that cycling . . .* ?

At 5pm we met up with James and Sarah to grab a bite to eat before heading back to the, sorry, Le Pub. Our overeager waiter was keen to ensure that we were as happy as could be with his service and the food and he soon began asking the obvious questions, trying to discuss with James whereabouts he was from. I was glad to be out of the firing line for once, particularly as the lack of common language meant the conversation was not really going smoothly. The reprieve was short lived. He broke from convention and went straight for the jugular asking what approximated to 'Do you know Manchester football?' I paused, clutching a noodle in mid-air, which was a feat in itself given my lack of dexterity with chopsticks, but I was aware that all eyes were now on me. I had no real choice did I?

"Yes. I support them."

"Manchester?"

"Yes, do you like Manchester United?"

"Yes, good. Very good."

I braced myself for the inevitable, 'Wayne Rooney, Wayne Rooney' but it wasn't forthcoming. Instead I heard possibly the most unexpected line of all . . . "Darren Fletcher."

My noodle was no longer hovering, it was back on the plate, possibly next to my jaw. "Sorry?" The waiter's English, while obviously better than my Vietnamese, was not great, and so I naturally took it as a mistake.

"Darren, err, Fletcher."

"No, surely not?"

"I think he said 'Darren Fletcher'," James interjected.

"No, surely not?"

"I like Darren Fletcher." He had a full sentence, but it felt as though he should have been standing, and proceeding it with, 'my name is . . .' at his local dubious-quality-footballers addiction meeting. (In retrospect, this is perhaps a little harsh as Fletcher went on to perform way beyond his previous best in the 08/09 season.) Maybe this guy was the closest thing to a United fan that I'd met on this jaunt, he even had his own obscure liking for a fringe player.

"You like Darren Fletcher?" I pushed.

"Yes, Darren Fletcher." Surely Fletcher's name can never have been repeated so frequently. I was smiling, on the verge of laughing; he took this to be a good sign and delighted with himself, smiled back. But that was as far as it got.

"Are you watching the match tonight?" I continued, hoping that this would lead to an unparalleled insight into a local Hanoi gathering, but that was it. The wheels came off the conversation, and soon he was asking if the food was nice again; the language gap was clearly blocking any further insight. We finished up and headed off, while he continued to work, suggesting that he wasn't going to be watching the match himself.

He wasn't the only one. The bar was a disappointingly familiar scene filled with a lot of uninterested people just enjoying a Saturday night out. The game itself was, as expected, quite entertaining but a 1-1 draw was not a great result against 16th-placed Everton. The disheartening thing was that I thought Everton had been struggling, or at least I had the impression that they had been. I didn't know for sure. There is, as ever, only so much you can glean from just reading results. I'd only been gone for about a month, but it already felt as though I didn't really know what was going on in the season. Yes, I had now watched three consecutive United games, and was well positioned to comment on our form, but not so well on the opposition. It didn't feel right. I could already detect a sense of detachment from the game, and while that didn't necessarily manifest itself in my support of United, it felt like a diluted sense of understanding. I had for instance, momentarily forgotten that Carlos Queiroz was now manager of Portugal and had to make a concerted effort to remember it. I didn't like it.

I had gotten my United fix, and the nature of the result certainly proved that I was quite capable of getting pissed off with a wasted opportunity to rack up some points. We were always going to be playing catch-up this season with our additional commitments, and while our 'friends' up the East Lancs road weren't realistically going to take the title, it was easy to guess that the media was ready to get carried away by the false impression that their position in the table was creating.

I texted my brother at the end of the game, basically saying that we should have won it, asking what he thought. He was unsure as he hadn't secured an away ticket, and the game hadn't been on the TV back in

England (pubs pointing in the Scandinavian direction aside). In a way that made me feel a little better, was this perhaps a fringe benefit, being able to watch a game that had been moved on 'police advice', but in reality probably had the Asian audience to thank for an earlier kick-off?

After the game finished and Newcastle v Sunderland began, we chose to head elsewhere. Walking through the streets it was apparent that many more TVs had been tuned to the football, making our earlier 'quest' even more farcical. They were largely disregarded by the tourists they were targeting though, let alone the locals who happened to be in the area.

As Lance Armstrong zipped by, we made our way into a bar overlooking a market, where from the balcony I soon noticed an elderly Vietnamese gentleman watching the remainder of the north-east derby. Shortly afterwards I glanced up to see him taking in a Bayern Munich game. This was clearly a football fan and somebody worth trying to speak to. When I headed up to the bar the absence of an on-screen score offered an easy opportunity to strike up a conversation. Apparently it was 4-2.

"Do you support Bayern Munich?"

"Huh?"

"Do you like Bayern?"

"No. Premier League."

"Ah, good. Me too. Which team?"

"Arsenal, Liverpool, Manchester."

"I support Manchester United. Which is your favourite?"

"Manchester City. Manchester United." The first person to be able to differentiate between the two.

"Do you like Manchester United?"

"Wayne Rooney. Wayne Rooney." Oh for fuck's sake.

"Yes Wayne Rooney. Do you like him?"

"Liverpool."

"You like Liverpool?"

"Yes . . . Wayne Rooney." This time he threw in a thumbs up to convey his pleasure with the conversation. It was a little like talking to a Vietnamese Fonz, who had replaced his obsession with motorbikes and leather jackets with a love for a Manchester United forward and their arch-rivals. We parted company with a few more 'Fonzies', and I returned to the table to enjoy the closing of a day that set new records for the repetition of the names Wayne Rooney and Darren Fletcher.

HALONG BAY
West Ham (h) 2-0
UK time: 29/10/08, 20.00
Local time: 30/10/08, 03.00

HALONG Bay, literally meaning 'Descending Dragon bay', lies in north-east Vietnam, but is quite unlike Geordie-land. Thousands of limestone karsts and isles of varying sizes comprise this UNESCO world heritage site and while the largest and most frequented of these, Cat Ba Island, offers the opportunity for overnight stays, the only real way to explore the area is by spending a night or two on a boat. Obvious question number one: can you watch football on a boat?

I knew it'd be unlikely, but we only had a limited amount of time to make our passage through Vietnam, Cambodia and into Thailand to hit our flight out in four weeks' time, and sticking around dry land for the West Ham game would have meant another two nights in Hanoi. Additionally, the company we wanted to use had a trip leaving on the Tuesday morning, so with all this considered I took the decision for the first time on the trip to purposely miss a game. I say I, because I opted not to tell Clare there was a game coming up on the Wednesday night, knowing that she'd have pushed me to stick around to watch it. Whilst it'd be easy to say 'Great, that's what everyone wants to hear,' I knew that even her best intentions could have caused problems. The extra days in a place that neither of us was greatly enjoying, the time of the kick-off and the subsequent pressure to move too fast through coming places would have compromised a lot more than one night. It was a funny decision to have to make. I guess I knew that it'd come along eventually, but so early in the trip made me worry that it might become a regular occurrence. I had to admit that the game itself was also a factor. Had it been a bigger game then I would've have pounced on Clare's charitable view and had us bed-down in Hanoi a few more days, screw the consequences. But I already felt I was juggling my squad, realising that I should save making demands to watch games for when it really mattered. Naturally there's a greater sense of excitement and anticipation for the big matches, but what was troubling was the ease with which I adopted such a casual attitude to a less enticing fixture. It was exactly the sort of thing I would have criticised someone at home for. But then there was always the hope that there'd be a television on the boat.

There was a television on the boat. It was humungous. My interest was piqued until the crew provided a sneak preview of the signal quality by persisting with a Vietnamese soap opera that unless set in a snow storm forced the damning conclusion that there'd be no football. In the most forlorn hope I still persuaded the chef to give me a go on the remote on Wednesday evening. He didn't understand what I was looking for, but it was soon clear that none of the channels worked – a distinct lack of aerial or satellite dish appeared to be the problem.

My disappearance had Clare interested, and she enquired as to what I was doing. "Just trying to find the football, there's a game tonight."

"What a United one?" She demanded.

"Yep."

"Well, why didn't you say? We could have stayed in Hanoi or something." (Predictable!)

"We couldn't really, we haven't got enough time."

"We could've worked something out."

"Nah, that's why I didn't tell you, I thought you'd be pleased that I chose this instead?" I think she seemed impressed with the consideration that I'd given it, maybe I was capable of compromise after all, maybe this was a more mature me, a sign that I had wider horizons than the boundaries of a football pitch. I grabbed a beer, and went and sat on the front of the boat to sulk, and talk to a guy called Seb, about football.

He too had given up his season ticket, Wolves in his case, to go travelling for a year. Obviously he wasn't getting the opportunity to watch his club's games as I sort of was, but had reached a point after two months where he wasn't even getting the scores texted to him anymore. He decided to let go for a year, almost completely. That was mildly comforting, I was still actually feeling a bit guilty about the ease with which I'd resigned myself to missing this match, but I would still awake to see: '2-0, Ronaldo got both, and Berbatov did a ridiculous bit of skill to set one up', on my phone; I was still trying. The feelings of guilt were strange, I hadn't really done anything wrong, Rio Ferdinand was not declining to leave the dressing room because someone else was sat in my seat. It was a bit childish to feel like this. But what did Berbatov do? How amazing was it? What could it have looked like? I invented a piece of skill in my head to compensate.

HUÉ

Hull (h) 4-3
UK time: 01/11/08, 15.00
Local time: 01/11/08, 22.00

WE left sea-life behind after a few days of doing little more than eating, drinking and sitting, to return to Hanoi for a few hours' wait before catching, yes, another overnight train – this time to Hué, or the Welsh town of Hugh as I preferred to call it. It was Thursday evening, the weather was distinctly miserable, it was dull and it was raining. We whiled away some of the wait in an internet café, where I tried to procure the name of a place to watch the game against Hull in two days' time.

It was difficult. With an estimated population of just under 350,000 Hué would be by far the smallest place we'd been for a United game so far, discounting the boat's population of 15 or so. It would be a real test of the 'United brand'; how deep was its penetration? In Vietnam they really had no right to think it'd be that entrenched.

Unlike the club's relationship with other Asian countries, there was little evidence of similar efforts in Vietnam. Although a United branded Vietnam language site does exist, exploiting the Manutd.com domain, there has been little of the hand-holding seen elsewhere. While visits to relative near neighbours Malaysia, and of course China and Hong Kong, have been a part of United's pre-season itineraries in the recent past, Vietnam are yet to be deemed worthy of such a visit. It has been reported that the club have received invitations over the past couple of years from both the Vietnam Football Federation and the Bank for Investment and Development of Vietnam to play in exhibition matches, perhaps against AC Milan who have also been approached, but suggested dates have been within the Premier League calendar leaving only a lump cash sum to attract them.

Vietnam is ear-marked as one of Asia's emerging economies but for now the club appear happy to allow their partners, most significantly Budweiser, to put in the ground-work for them. The 'Bud 6v6 International Cup' offers the opportunity for six teams taken from tournaments in the country's two major cities (Hanoi and Ho Chi Minh) to play at Old Trafford. Walter Blocker, the CEO of Budweiser's authorised distributors in Vietnam believes: "Football is king in Vietnam. It's everyone's dream to play at Old Trafford." Although grand total entries of 500 teams, narrowed to 64 for the tournament, hardly suggests a clamour to live that dream.

Huế was baking hot, the rain that had been falling in Hanoi was a distant memory, but there didn't seem to be much to the place. Clare was busy frowning on my decision for us to stay for two nights, while I was busy sweating. The bars seemed confined to a solitary street, along with most of the traveller accommodation, so it seemed unlikely that there'd be any interesting places to watch the Hull game, if any at all. I did have a back-up plan on this occasion though, as we had a television in our room, complete with Star Sports.

One of my developing concerns was how a lack of day-to-day contact with football and the sports media available in the UK was diluting my sense of the season, and that travelling was creating a unique bubble in which I was basically supporting the club alone. My lack of realisation that this apprehension should have spread deeper and further was brutally exposed on the morning of the Hull game, as the rain that we had left behind in Hanoi came flooding back into our consciousness. By chance, on our way back into our hostel that afternoon, after a carefree day at beach, we glanced over the shoulder of a Vietnamese woman at a computer and saw she was viewing photos of cars window-deep in water; a member of staff was staring at a television set showing similar images. We fired up another computer to investigate and soon discovered what we were lucky to have escaped. Over the course of Friday and early Saturday Hanoi had experienced its hardest rain in 35 years, which had led to the death of at least 92 people, and countless damage to homes and businesses.

It was difficult to comprehend the starkness of the tragedy and our proximity to it. Unsurprisingly there was a measure of relief that we'd not been caught up in it, having just experienced what was the start of the rainfall, but we had avoided it by just 24 hours. The speed and level of devastation was hard to take in, particularly as our Englishness meant natural disasters barely register as a day-to-day concern. It just didn't seem plausible, and our ignorance of events up to then hardened the feelings of guilt and deflation that the realisation brought. The ideals of travelling and the liberating disconnection that can bring was previously being compromised by my football diet, yet this clearly called into question the wisdom of a media-void on all levels. While the passage that we were taking was endlessly broadening our horizons, it was apparent that the language barrier prevented the natural osmosis of information that the media barrage in England fed and was capable of leaving us disengaged very easily. It became imperative to track this news now, not just because of the level of the tragedy, but because the rain was heading in our direction.

A balance of sympathy and respect was obviously called for; we were far less a part of the tragedy than any of the Vietnamese people, and to try and pretend otherwise would be hugely insolent, but similarly getting drunk and shouting at a TV set was not appropriate. Clare was feeling ill, but was eager to get out for a bit, so we made our way to the DMZ café at the end of the road, the most likely venue for the football. A conversation with the manager didn't shed much light on whether they'd show the match, and he asked us to come back in a few hours. We went for a quick bite to eat, which pushed Clare over the edge, and after a couple of visits to the facilities, I played the caring boyfriend and decided that our room was the best place for us.

Admittedly I'd been looking for an excuse to watch the game in comfort ever since finding the right TV channel. Huế was not going to help me get closer to any Vietnamese United fans and the chance to watch a game in peace would be pleasant. So, we returned to our falsified bubble, where Premier League football was important, and natural disasters took a back seat. It was nice to watch the game like this, fully focused on the football. The only interruptions I had to contend with were Clare's intermittent dashes to the toilet, as she took the honours as the first of us to succumb to 'traveller's diarrhoea' – the shits – and the barrage of Tiger beer adverts that kept dropping onto the screen.

As a 3pm kick-off it was another game available to an Asian television audience but not an English one, and in fact it'd become clear that every United league game was televised. An entertaining 4-3 provided a nice distraction from the real-life events being shown on other channels and brought a strange realisation. Up to now my attendance at games had made football my real-life events, had they suddenly become secondary? Playing Hull, let's face it a pretend Premier League team, and in a goal-fest only added to the lack of seriousness of the events; it felt carefree. Was my lack of ability to see an element of seriousness or intrigue in the game evidence that I was attaching less importance to the sport?

HO CHI MINH CITY
Celtic (a) 1-1
UK time: 05/11/08, 19.45
Local time: 06/11/08, 02.45

BY the time the Celtic game came around in the early hours of Thursday morning, we'd been back in the swing of big city living for a couple of days, and were fully dosed up on propaganda. Demarcation of Vietnam during the conflict means that the large majority of 'war attractions' are based in and around Ho Chi Minh City, with the onus very much on the presentation of 'America the savage'. The War Remnants Museum is a powerful and often harrowing depiction of victims of chemical attacks in particular, but the Chi Chu Tunnels, part of the underground network used by the Vietcong in the conflict, has become a somewhat farcical monument to a tourist playground taking precedence over any political or historical agenda.

On the day of United's Champions League group stage visit to Celtic Park, we got up early to catch a bus for the 90-minute trip out to the tunnels. Upon arrival an initiation video sets the scene, and it's hard not to chuckle as the American soldiers' actions are portrayed as that of "crazed devils, they shot at buildings, pots and pans, schools and even the grass."

Having established that the US is inhabited by the slightly unhinged cousins of Beelzebub, there followed a short tour of the tunnel complex, working demonstrations of various mantraps of which each station guide was incredibly proud, and a quick crawl through the ludicrously claustrophobic tunnels before we were offered the opportunity to pay to fire various weapons, from handguns to AK-47 assault rifles. There were plenty of Americans around so the grass was probably shitting it; I certainly spotted a pensive wok.

It was something that just didn't appeal to me. I had known it was 'an activity' offered at the tunnels, and various other places throughout south-east Asia (indeed a friend had once recounted a tale of an American in Cambodia asking how much it'd cost to put a grenade in a pig), but I was still amazed by the level of interest there was. It was particularly disturbing to see the father of a South African family rhetorically ask his wife and two teenage sons: "Are we all gonna shoot together?" before adding the familiar rallying cry: "Shall we go for machine guns?" Families often complain that days out as a unit are too expensive, and I could see their point. Is it reasonable for a family of four to be expected to pay around $200 just to pump lead into the ether? No wonder family values are under threat. It was this money-spinner that really tarnished any impact the historical site might have had and made motives for attendance questionable.

I overheard an Australian guy explaining to a girl he'd been painfully haranguing all day that: "you had to do it to feel like a man." It may have come from cross-cultural distortion but my lack of gun-toting action was not making me feel less manful, besides I was going to drink some beer and watch football at 2.45 in the morning later on, so I had plenty of chances to score on that scale. To ensure my masculinity was up to it we went for a quick nap when we got back just to make sure there was no stroppiness to come when heads got tired, and a little like a kid on New Years Eve I was rested up.

I did still have hopes for Vietnam; the imagery in Hanoi and the fake goods available were good signs. Ho Chi Minh was also a big city providing our final stop in the country and a last chance to bump into United watchers. Still, it was going to be 4.30am when it finished, and a clear state of drunkenness would be needed to make it to that time, not the best way to pay proper attention to a football match. This mental struggle was clearly etched on my face as I stared lovingly at the television in the corner. "What are you thinking about?" Clare demanded.

"Erm..."

"You're not watching it here, come on, you're going," she added, evidently keener to meet these potential United fans then I was, or possibly just eager to go out rather than sit in a dingy room and watch *Kindergarten Cop* before some football hours later. Was that not what travelling was all about? It looked as though we were definitely going. Damn, what happened to those days of illness?

The Blue Gecko bar, a 30-minute walk from the Pham Ngu Lao area was our first effort. A bar away from tourist central could be more of a locals' haunt perhaps – not when it turns out to be a tacky Australian bar though. A few drinks and an hour of Clare singing power ballads was enough, so we headed back towards Pham Ngu Lao. Ho Chi Minh late night is a lively place with bars quite thickly condensed; it feels vibrant and more interesting than Hanoi. The problem for my search was that the revellers were mostly tourists, plenty of them, but just tourists. We settled on the Goto Pub right on the corner of De Tham Street, but as the match neared the people thinned out and there was no sign of any 'United fans'. Asking at the bar revealed it would close between 4 and 5am, thus part way through the game and as we were both drunk, a recurring matchday theme it seemed, we decided to head back. There was simply no point in watching the game here. It was frustrating and beginning to feel like all I was doing was compiling a list of pubs you can watch football in abroad.

After ten minutes ringing the bell, and banging on the door, the sleepy nightstaff let us in five minutes after kick-off. Clare was soon asleep, but I was rather impressed that I managed to stay awake for the whole game – although bouts of standing up and washing my face were needed to make it to 4.30am. The game wasn't exhilarating by any means, the team lacked fluency. In fact things felt scrappy on many levels; the games, the ways they were being watched and the places they were being watched in. It all felt a little like a struggle. There was no part of me that wanted to stop watching the games, but I was not looking forward to match days at all. Although Clare was there with me, she simply wasn't interested in the games, and had slept through the last two. It felt very much like a solitary pursuit. I'd always thought that a supporter's relationship with the club was relatively lonely, at least very personal, and expressed differently for every individual, but this lack of connection was a problem, and that was surprising me. I'd expected things to become more United-centric throughout Vietnam, my first real exposure to large amounts of coverage through easy access to television, but the club weren't even pushing themselves as hard as Arsenal, who had their faces on a brand of shower gel and deodorant called 'Hat-trick'. They seemed anonymous in everyday life, and things seemed unlikely to get any better as we headed for the neighbouring and more-impoverished Cambodia.

Cambodia

PHNOM PENH
Arsenal (a) 1-2
UK time: 08/11/08, 12.45
Local time: 08/11/08, 19.45

A REAL GAME. A nice top-four dust-up. This was going to be enjoyable. My football spirits were certainly recharged; forget what I'd said about not looking forward to the matches, I most certainly was. We weren't playing superbly by any means but niggling injuries and fixture scheduling were contriving to knock us out of stride, so this was exactly the sort of match we needed to get us back on track and remind people that we were the best team in the country (England not Cambodia). Arsenal were struggling themselves, with rumours swirling around (the internet, not Cambodia) that Arsène Wenger may even quit. It all made for a potentially jovial occasion.

After my lack of success hunting down local United fans, I'd decided back in Ho Chi Minh that contacting a few local media outlets ahead of our arrival in Cambodia may help. At worst it could put me in touch with someone on the ground who had an idea what was really going on, and they may be interested in what I was doing. I didn't receive any replies, but thought the short notice could well have been responsible for that. In the absence of the insider information I'd hoped for, the 'Gym Bar' seemed the only sports pub in town so was the likely venue for our custom come Saturday.

Cambodia, Phnom Penh in particular, is the most emotionally draining place I have ever visited. To travel for a long period of time, without much money, leads to you becoming pretty tight with your cash. You have to get used to shrugging off attempts to sell you tat that you don't need, and resist the temptation to give money to everyone who asks for it. In some cases it's hard to do, but turning a blind eye becomes second-nature (questionably). In Cambodia though, you find yourself buying a drink from a shop, taking a sip and then giving it away to a child within seconds.

Digesting the reality of a country still very much in the shadow of the Khmer Rouge rule that led to the genocidal killing of up to a fifth of its entire population (between one and two million people) is very difficult when you are placed so close to the long lasting effects. The two major monuments to these horrors, the Killing Fields and the Tuol Sleng Museum (the former school converted to the notorious S-21 'genocide' prison), are unlikely to appear in anyone's top ten world-wide attractions because of their nature, but they remain the bleakest and most frighteningly educational experience of our trip.

A matchday morning might begin with a lie-in after a night-out, before a slow breakfast, a browse of the newspaper or the internet for latest team news, a little bet or a beer perhaps; all part of the ritualistic waiting for the most eagerly anticipated 90 minutes of the weekend. A visit to the Tuol Sleng museum was certainly not the usual appetiser for a Premier League football match.

The museum houses the most engrossing and powerful photographic exhibition I've ever seen. I'm not usually the most patient of museum viewers, and can rip through most 'tourist attractions' in about a fifth of the suggested time; not so here. To a man, our fellow visitors shared the same grave countenance, bemused disbelief etched across their faces. We spent two hours in total silence, weaving through the former classrooms, trying to absorb the level of atrocity that the pictures and words laid out before us portrayed. There is no part of the museum that is enjoyable and it's hard to know how to act when confronted with such horror, but you feel compelled to harden your frown and continue the education.

When we left, heads bowed, our tuk-tuk driver, Olas, (clearly the coolest driver in town on account of his camouflage visor and aviators) casually threw in: "So shall we go to the Killing Fields now?" We decided to leave that trip until the next day, but it was the casual nature of his comment that was remarkable, exemplifying Cambodian resilience in the face of such recent tragic history. It can be hard to know how to act at times around such sensitive issues, but the warmth with which the people greet you and the positivity of their attitude enables you to feel at ease and able to enjoy your stay in the country.

What was striking, endearing, commendable – call it what you will – was the dramatic difference in the presentation of the respective histories of the outward looking Vietnam and the introspective Cambodia. That soul-searching, that capacity for self-examination made it all the more poignant; a testimony to the humble nature of a people whose position doesn't afford them the luxury of unnecessary procrastination and the chance to dwell. They simply have to get on with it.

Against that backdrop of a war ravaged past and the current evident poverty that has left the country a target for sex-tourists (indeed, hideously, World Vision estimate a third of prostitutes are children), it feels wrong that football should really matter. That in a few hours we were going to watch a football match, one from the richest league in the world, between Manchester United and Arsenal, being played at the Emirates Stadium, and thus one of the largest displays of opulence from the safety of the western world seemed a little farcical.

The Gym Bar was yet again another western sports bar, replete with football shirted walls and imported beer on tap. It was full of westerners there merely to while away their Saturday watching football and drinking and consequently my notion that there'd be locals too made me feel ashamedly naïve. The contrasts between the world inside the pub and that on the other side of the door were immense. But on the one hand, while I realised there were obviously more important things for people to think about given the levels of poverty that had confronted us on every corner for the last day and a half, perhaps it was the escapism of something like the Premier League that helped facilitate the forward-looking positivity that permeated the country. In fact would the Manchester United brand, and the life-affirming principles and ideals it often espouses, that freshness of youth and physical health, not be more valuable here than anywhere? Is sport, and football in particular, not used across the world in that way by millions every week, providing a chance to escape the daily grind?

All that considered, did that not just make part of what I was doing even more lamentable? If I was to happen across a Cambodian United fan in the bar, if he was deemed good enough to temporarily inhabit this little bit of England, then was it not utterly ridiculous for me to start haranguing him and questioning him on what the hell he was thinking using my football club to provide a further measure of hope and escapism from the brutal reality of life on the streets of Phnom Penh? Was I really that ridiculous? Was I really that much of a conceited arsehole? Surely I was bigger than that, had more perspective? It might matter to me as part of my life at home, but surely not in all circumstances? Should I not instead be happy that something that brings endless joy to me was also capable of lighting up other parts of the planet, and in fact be proud that it was United, with their distinctive history and attacking philosophy, that was doing it rather than another side?

Furthermore, if United really wanted to play the good guys in all this, shouldn't they be travelling to somewhere like Cambodia as part of their tour – taking one step out of their money-spinning itinerary to go some-where it would really make a difference? Football does have that healing power, that ability to help people move on and embrace new cultures and new beginnings. Should they not be driving that? Or was that just naïvety at work again?

By kick-off the bar was packed. This was easily the biggest turnout for a game I'd experienced since being away and it was like being in a pub back home, aside from the number of Americans. No locals though, well at least not at first. Shortly before half-time with Arsenal leading 1-0, a guy came in and sat a short way in front of us. He was clearly revelling in the atmos-phere, cheering everything United did as they sought to get back in the game. He seemed the happiest man present by quite a long way, full of little yelps and leaps from his stool, constantly looking back to us for approval for his giddy acts. It was tough not to laugh, which as with any errant middle-aged Cambodian only served to encourage him.

I thought a more casual chat about United in general would be okay later, leaving him to enjoy his food at half-time. The second half soon kicked-off and when Samir Nasri put Arsenal two up I was starting to get a bit pissed off, but the crazy little guy in front was jumping up and down shouting "Arsenal, Arsenal". What was happening here? Did he just want football to be the winner? I was still ready to talk to him come full-time though, even if just to find out what the hell was going on, but it must've quickly gotten too much for him as he shot out the door ten minutes later.

The boisterousness of the remaining English was being matched by the pub's adequate quota of 'crazed devils', who perhaps failed to realise that all sport is not produced merely for them. It was with little glee that I anticipated watching matches in America in four months' time given the ludicrous nature of many a comment. Particularly galling was when one within earshot said: "It's great to see Scholes, what a legend" when Ryan Giggs came on as sub. *You are allowed to just stay quiet,* I think. The weather clearly cottoned on to what was happening as it began pissing it down straight after the game, so at 10pm we decided to go back. This wasn't a day for joviality.

It turned out to be our one and only game in Cambodia. Our trip to Siem Reap, to the Temples of Angkor, should have been punctuated by a League Cup tie with QPR, but it seems the blasé attitude to the competition that persists in England pervades Asia too as it was omitted from the television schedules. I was a little bit glad. It was another silly time, and in all likelihood we would put out a severely weakened side and either lose to the evident glee of the commentary team or scrape our way through. It was the first time that we'd had no control over proceedings whatsoever, it had been taken out of our hands, and it was a rather liberating feeling.

Our time in Cambodia was certainly thought provoking, and reflecting on that later, its lasting effect on a personal level remains strong. It's an enjoyable country to visit where the resolve of the people is impressive and the supposed 'crime' of supporting a team from another part of the world had all seemed a little pathetic. Perhaps my appreciation of circumstance and the value of the global reach of United was changing.

Thailand

BANGKOK

Stoke (h) 5-0
UK time: 15/11/08, 15.00
Local time: 15/11/08, 22.00

BANGKOK, THE BIGGEST tourist whore of all, only made it on to our itinerary because its Suvarnabhumi airport is the major transport hub of south-east Asia, and our only option for a flight to Tokyo. However, the recent ownership of Manchester City by Thaksin Shinawatra (he'd sold it the previous August) made it an interesting proposition for me. Having rather surprisingly passed the Premier League's 'fit and proper person test', and been portrayed in sections of the British media as a much loved figurehead back home, it was reasonable to think that perhaps there'd be a City shirt or two knocking around as a calling card of support from his countrymen.

In truth Shinawatra polarised opinion in Thailand, rising to power on an election bid backed by big business and charming the less affluent, but leaving him generally abhorred by the middle classes. Alienating the modern-day Premier League's key demographic, targeted abroad for their buying 'legitimate goods' power and tendency to hop on the football bandwagon, didn't sit too well with his purchase of City. Consequently, given his exile, was it not reasonable to think that while the former Thai leader's sale of United's neighbours back in August 2008 was in part due to his assets being frozen at home, it was also evidence that short-term ownership of the club was his only consideration – his regular attendance at matches providing a clever way of subverting the censorship of a media controlled by the military government that ousted him and frequently getting his face on television back home. If true, to any extent, then it's certainly telling of his belief in the reach of Premier League broadcasts.

When Asian markets are covered in discussions involving United it is Japan, China, Malaysia and South Korea that usually figure highly. Thailand, at least in the recent past, is not usually amongst them, although during the club's 2001 tour Peter Kenyon ridiculously claimed that of the 8 million inhabitants of Bangkok, 1.8 million were United fans. But let's face it, he also identified himself as one. However, they were making inroads here ahead of rivals (United were busy opening a club branded bar in a hotel while City were shutting down 'operations' in the country as 2008 came to a close) and their commercial presence was startlingly obvious on just the drive from the airport. First up was an imposing billboard advert partnering the team with Smirnoff under the tagline 'Spirit of Champions' (a campaign that is behind the appearance of the 'United against drink driving' banners that have popped-up pitch-side lately), a surprising affiliation given their hypersensitivity over image. Next was a roadside ad for one of United's own products: the Manchester United credit card (which incidentally as well as in the UK and Hong Kong is also available in Poland for some reason). As good a test of loyalty as any other I guess – if you're willing to trust your debt management to the Glazers then you're pretty much going to sign up for anything the club could think up: Fergie's anger management classes co-chaired by Roy Keane? Mike Phelan's DVD: *Why trousers are bad*, anyone? Or perhaps a football who-dunnit penned by Steve Bruce? . . . Oh.

Bangkok was clearly a different commercial entity, maybe somewhere a major British supermarket chain would not seem out of place. "Oh look there's a Tesco," Clare idly announced, interrupting my thoughts. Was this what Thailand's capital was all about? We hadn't even had a whiff of a ladyboy but we'd seen a bloody Tesco. As we made our way downtown, and the traffic got thicker, I noticed a few United bumper stickers floating around. Perhaps it wasn't just United as big business around here, maybe there were fans on the ground interested in the actual football of all things.

I couldn't find the game listed on television schedules on the internet, but had seen it advertised outside bars around Khao San Road (the infamous centre of Thai tourist debauchery) the day before so thought that returning there would be the best bet. After six weeks on the road we were frankly sick of the sight of sights, and had thus decided that we weren't going to do anything more than relax in Bangkok, and with no decent accommodation available in the Khao San area we'd opted for a bit more affordable comfort a short taxi ride away. So come matchnight we jumped in a cab, then jumped out again when he refused to take us on the meter and wanted five times the real price, then jumped in and out of a second cab, before finding a third that was willing to play by the rules.

The rules unfortunately seemed to involve driving into the thickest possible traffic and following a series of diversions before coming to a halt at a police roadblock. We had no idea what was really going on, but it was clear that the taxi driver wanted us out of his car because he was being forced to turn around. He gave us a half-hearted point in one direction which wasn't very helpful – good luck getting a taxi in Beijing pal – and we got out none the wiser about what was happening. What's that? Lost again? Yep.

There were lots of people around so we assumed we couldn't be too far away from the action and gambled on the general direction of the point. It soon felt like a bad punt, so we headed back from where we'd come to find the volume of people increasing all the time. There were crowds of locals of all ages, from children to octogenarians, but all similarly dressed; smartly with black a common theme. This couldn't be the makings of a standard Saturday night-out in Bangkok surely? What was this, a ceremony of some sort? People dispersing from a parade?

We soon made it back to Khao San Road; at the top end there was another swell of what increasingly looked like mourners, but in the main people seemed as oblivious to what was going on as we did. Liverpool's 12.45pm game was taking place, proving football was being shown in a number of bars and leaving us in a 'take your pick' situation. On account of it having the most people sitting outside, the biggest screen and the cheapest Thai buckets (basically a chance to drink a combination of Thai whisky, Coke and Red Bull from a bucket more frequently associated with the construction of sandcastles) we chose a bar that had been converted, in the loosest sense of the word – you sat on the forecourt – from a petrol station.

We waited until the early game had finished to ensure any 'vermin' had cleared out before taking our seats. The bar was beginning to fill up as kick-off neared, and amazingly sat a short way behind us were a group of three Thais, two of which were wearing Manchester United shirts. This was it, at last. Finally, I'd found some fans in their natural habitat, going out of their way to watch games in a public place. Maybe it was the more accommodating time-slot, maybe it was the easy access to alcohol, or maybe it was just luck, but at least they were there.

Shit, that of course meant that I was going to have to speak to them. I wasn't just going to have to speak to them, I was going to have to randomly go up to a group of people and out of nowhere pursue, in a foreign tongue, what amounted to a mildly aggressive line of questioning, only pausing to sip on a viscous cocktail of alcohol using a child's beach toy as its vessel. This was going to test my 'journalistic instinct' to the full. Problem was, I didn't really have any, and didn't have a clue what I was going to ask them.

"Wow, there's actually some United fans behind you Tim," Clare said midway through a slurp from her bucket.

"Yep."

"Go and talk them then." I smiled rather pathetically in response. "What? No chance. I'm not going for you, that's ridiculous."

"That's a definite no then?"

"Yes, that's a definite no."

"Ok. What do you think I should say?"

"I don't bloody know."

"Ok. I think I'll leave it till half-time. It's not like they're going to leave is it?"

"Just like the crazy guy in Phnom Penh didn't leave?"

"This is different, they've just turned up, they're here to watch the game. They're . . . you know . . . here for football."

"Did you almost say they're 'United fans'?"

"No. I'm leaving it till half-time anyway. Don't shake your head at me, especially whilst drinking out of a bucket. There's only five minutes till kick-off, I'll speak to them at half-time." That would at least give me time to think of some questions, hopefully. This black cloud of impending doom was going to ruin the first half wasn't it? If there was to be a first half that is. The channel was suddenly changed; where a United procession had been about to start, a funeral procession now reigned, providing a handy link to the mourners we'd seen. But, come on, how important could it be? This was a Saturday night, who'd want to watch it anyway? Damn, it looked like a state funeral – this was going to be problematic.

Thailand loves its royal family to an extent I've never seen anywhere else in the world. Like a royal Edson Arantes do Nascimento, or Pelé, the current head of state, 81-year-old Phra Bat Somdet Phra Poramintharamaha Bhumibol Adulyadej Mahitalathibet Ramathibodi Chakkrinaruebodin Sayamminthrathirat Borommanatbophit, goes by a more digestible moniker: Bhumibol Adulyadej, and receives an unconditional love from all quarters, that needs to be seen to be believed.

A simple visit to the cinema can confirm this for anyone, and did so for us the day before the match. It's not your average trailers that provide the film's appetiser here, instead you are required to rise with the national anthem blaring from the Dolby Sound System as an accompanying montage of the King meeting and greeting his people in his younger days flickers across the silver screen. This paying of respects is taken very seriously by fellow cinemagoers who are on their feet in seconds with any tardiness frowned upon. Thankfully you are allowed to return to your seat for the actual film. But still, that is nothing compared to the peculiar scene we encountered during rush-hour at one of Bangkok's 'air-train' stations.

People scurrying in all directions, bursting to reach the sanctity of their homes after a gruelling day's work, were brought to a sudden and immediate halt as the national anthem suddenly boomed from the station's PA system. Silence spread almost instantly across the concourse, shrouding the platforms and shooting up and down the escalators as commuters froze on the spot leaving only the regal anthemic tones, and Clare's rabbiting filling the air. Her back was turned to the action as she continued obliviously pumping money into the ticket machine. She must notice, she'd surely realise that no-one else was so much as moving, let alone carrying out a financial transaction. Apparently not, I was going to have to break silence too, through gritted teeth mind: "Clare, shut up. Keep still. Nobody's moving. You're going to get us killed." Finally she came to a halt under the glare of the station guards. Moments later the music stopped, releasing those caught in mid-stride from their cryogenic state, allowing them to go on their way as though it was the most normal thing in the world.

So, as imported football product was replaced by televised state funeral, I didn't exactly fancy my chances of getting things reversed. It had all been too easy here, too good to be true. In just three or so minutes since the channel had been changed a group of onlookers had gathered at the back of the forecourt; but come on, these weren't drinkers – think business goddammit. The screen flickered back to the match, the line-ups were showing, it was almost time to go. But a tantalising 30-second glimpse was all we were getting before it was all doom and gloom once more. One of the shirted fans behind me was up-in-arms. "Hey!" he shouted indiscriminately into the air, it being much harder to direct your complaints to management when there is no conceivable bar, rather a piece of tarpaulin, a few Portaloos and a scattering of rats. "Hey," he screamed again. I was beginning to like him, he was prepared to kick up a fuss; which in the circumstances was either very brave or very stupid.

As well as being more popular than your average Joe, the King is also protected by Lèse Majesté law (which roughly translates in English to 'injury to majesty'), whereby anyone, including foreigners, insulting or questioning him is liable to serve a prison term. This is not one of those absurd ancient laws that exist in many a constitution and organically become defunct, such as the British law permitting the murder of a Scotsman within the ancient city walls of York, as long as he is carrying a bow and arrow. (Just that meteoric rise from the conference to engineer with York City now, huh Rafa?) No, this law is alive and kicking and rigorously enforced to this day. For example, Frenchman Lech Tomasz Kisielewicz was jailed for two weeks upon landing in Bangkok in 2005 for refusing to turn off a reading light on a plane he had been sharing with two Thai Princesses. A Swiss man, Oliver Jufer, was sentenced to ten years in jail for the drunken act of daubing black paint on the King's face in a portrait, and finally, causing me to tread a little more carefully, is the tale of Australian Harry Nicolaides who was sentenced to three years in jail in January 2009 after being charged with Lèse Majesté because of a passage in his book, which is thought to have only sold about a dozen copies. He was however pardoned by the King and released a month later. Furthermore Lèse Majesté has led to access to websites such as YouTube being blocked nationwide, while criminal complaints often relate to people failing to stand in the cinema, and possibly now for nattering at the ticket machine in the train station.

All in all this guy was taking a risk. This was, as it turned out, the cremation of Princess Galyani Vadhana, the King's sister (who had died the previous January, strangely 11 months prior to her official state cremation), whose death had in fact indirectly led to Lèse Majesté being enforced before when the website of Same Sky Books was shut down by the government because of comments on a forum querying Thai media for claiming the whole country was in mourning over her passing. Despite this, amazingly his protests worked. Someone flicked it back with just 30 seconds on the clock. It was football time.

Having avoided arrest for their disrespect the three fans were still sat behind us come half-time, so now it was time for me to spring into action. I reached their table and realised that an introduction was going to be necessary: "Hi, do you speak English?"

"A little bit," one of them replied, who I took to be the most fluent.

"Hi, I just wanted to speak to you about being Manchester United fans." A small nod of acknowledgement. A westerner at another table shifted in his seat to look across at what was going on. "Why do you support the team?"

"Erm . . . because of Eric Cantona, the first time." I was unsure what the first time meant.

"And what about your friends?" I pushed.

They spoke in Thai for a couple of seconds, but he didn't reply, he just looked at me. They weren't warming to me. I told him about my attempts to meet United fans, told him where I was from and what I was doing. He shrugged his shoulders, and looked at me again. What, was that it? What happens now? I'd kind of assumed that people would just talk when I asked them questions, isn't that how conversations normally work? "Ok, thanks," I said walking away wondering when exactly Jeremy Paxman would contact me for tips.

"That was an absolute failure."

"Was it? Why? You weren't there for very long."

"Yep. Fancy trying to get a photo?"

"Not really."

"Go on I'll be in it, if you take it."

At full-time we intercepted one of them, cleverly targetting a non-English speaker so that it was more difficult for him to object, documenting evidence of the worst interview of all time. I hadn't wanted to come to Bangkok in the first place anyway. I knew it'd be rubbish, and in fact we made it out just in time, leaving for Tokyo just a couple of days before anti-government protesters closed the airport for over a week.

Japan

TOKYO
Aston Villa (a) 0-0
UK time: 22/11/08, 17.30
Local time: 23/11/08, 02.30

Villarreal (a) 0-0
UK time: 25/11/08, 19.45
Local time: 26/11/08, 04.45

JAPAN WAS MY most eagerly anticipated destination of our entire trip. I wasn't entirely sure why but was definitely finding that I preferred big city living to rural authenticity and so perhaps the lure of Tokyo was behind it. It wasn't that Land of the Rising Sun allure that intrigued me though, it was more the *Back to the Future II* of hover-boards and holographic theatres that I was hoping for. However, in some ways, I knew this could be our toughest stop of the lot - not only a big 'culture shock', and hugely expensive in a trip of this ilk, but also the most gruelling time zone (being nine hours ahead) from a United perspective.

The potential expense of a visit to Japan had been a bit of a concern all along, but putting together a rough itinerary early the previous May, we'd decided that if we were tight with our budget in the cheaper countries, avoided the crowded Christmas period, and stayed for only eight or nine days we'd be alright. Two things altered the perception of our ideal time to go. One was United winning the Champions League and consequently being scheduled to play in the Club World Cup in Japan just a month later than our visit (a source of constant annoyance that I hadn't had the foresight to realise – the £1,000 each it would have cost us to re-route our trip around it was just too much) and the second was the pound flopping dramatically. We'd previously been pretty happy to be away from the doom and gloom that seemed to be engulfing England as the recession kicked in, initially thinking it meant we'd avoid a lot of the consequences ('Japan's not as expensive as you think,' *Lonely Planet* boldly predicts. No, it's a lot worse than that). But the exchange rate had slipped from 220 yen to the pound, back in May, to just 138 by the time we arrived.

Accommodation was also hard to find. We'd been advised that it booked up quickly in Japan, in fact months in advance, but took that to be just another clichéd sound-bite along the lines of 'the earlier you book the better'. We'd not had any trouble up to now, so why expect things to change? Playing it a little safe we started trying to find something reasonably priced once we got to Bangkok, but it wasn't until we were leaving the city after hours on the internet that we finally had things sorted. By sorted, I mean staying for one night in a dorm in Tokyo, before two nights in a dorm in Kyoto, followed by two nights in a tiny studio flat miles out of the centre of Tokyo, before returning to the original hostel for the final three – all with no single night costing less than 70 per cent of our daily budget. Turns out the warnings were correct then.

What was instantly noticeable upon arrival at the hostel apart from the presence of an English man outside training to be a sumo wrestler (seriously) was just how glum everyone inside was. Maybe it was because it was a bit chilly, or that they couldn't afford to do anything because they had no money left and were consequently being forced to eat freeze-dried noodles for every meal, but everyone was so bloody miserable – aside from the guy outside screaming as he stamped barefoot on the concrete in an attempt to harden the bottom of his feet for the battle that awaited. He was loving it. Everything was instantly a little bit unusual, but brilliantly so.

The streets were amazingly clean, nearly all of them flanked by vending machines that leave you never more than 100 yards away from a drink of water (supposedly there's one machine for every 23 people), it felt eerily-still like a film set, and it delivered on so many levels. The food, perhaps not so accessible to the budget traveller was nevertheless enticing; sushi of course, but even giblet soup tasted nice here. The 80s fascination with futuristic Japanese toilets also rang true. From our cold accommodation, and boring bathrooms, a trip to the facilities in a shopping centre was an event in itself. It was pleasurable. It was cold outside. In the privacy of a cubicle it was warm; you could adjust the seat height; tailor the temperature of your throne; dry yourself; wash yourself in different ways – a gentle spray perhaps or is a more pressurised water-jet to your liking? – all at the touch of a button. There were so many varied combinations to try that no two visits were the same, thankfully. After all I certainly didn't want to repeat a certain scolding I received from an over-exuberant use of the hot water squirter. The toilet experience kind of summed up the exciting depth of Tokyo life.

With reservations fully committing us to a trip to Kyoto the following day we made our way, via a couple of toilet stops, to the station to buy some train tickets. We knew it would be another big expense, but there were, it seemed, two kinds of train, and while the world famous Bullet Train was the more appealing it was certainly not going to be the cheapest. The use of calculators as international translators came to the fore as the women behind the desk typed 12,710 into a calculator and handed it to us: "What! That's about 4,000 yen more than we thought, isn't it?" I said, beginning to think that we were to be financially ruined in the space of a few days.

"Erm, yeah I think so," Clare replied, clutching the guidebook, "that's what it says here anyway."

"Show her the book." We pointed to the 'limited express' – the cheaper train listed. She nodded and smiled. Okay good, I thought.

After a pause she pointed to the calculator again, saying: "Only Shinkansen."

"Only Shinkansen?" I asked.

"Only Shinkansen."

"Express?" I looked forlornly to the book.

"Express. No. Only Shinkansen."

"Only Shinkansen?" Her nodding sufficed this time. "I think there's only Shinkansen."

"Yeah I got that, thanks Tim." Clare stared at me. "What does it mean?"

"I think it means Bullet Train and so much more expensive."

"Damn, we've got no choice though. We've paid for accommodation. And we did kinda want to go on the Bullet Train." Yes, we'd got to the point where we felt the need to fully test the rail capabilities of a country now, and I was actually a little bit excited by travelling on a train that looked like it was straight out of the *Jetsons* cartoon. What was becoming of me?

"Yep ok. That's just for one person, yes?" I asked with accompanying hand signals. She nodded in confirmation.

"How much is that then?" Clare asked. I reached for the calculator and did the simple but horrifying sums.

"Yeah, quite a lot." It was £92 "But what else can we do?"

"Two returns please," we asked.

"Return?"

"Err, yeah, there and back please." Conversations in Japan were already proving tough, and this was with the English speaker of the office. "To Kyoto, and from Kyoto."

"Erm…"

"Does this get us to Kyoto and back to Tokyo?"

"You want to come to Tokyo."

"Yes."

"This just to Kyoto."

"Really? How much is a return?" She went to the calculator, but the sum looked less than complicated, and the 25,420 on the display confirmed she'd merely multiplied it by two.

"So it's gonna cost us £368, just for the train?" Clare announced after a dabble on the keys. "What's our budget again?"

"Bollocks. We're just going to have to pay. There's no point in reserving a seat though, 'cos if we miss the train we're screwed, and there's no point in buying a return cos if we lose half of it then we're screwed. And I wish she'd stop smiling at us."

"She's just friendly, everyone here is. I love it."

"Well you better love it when we're eating pot noodles for the next ten days too. No wonder all the travellers are so miserable."

It was abundantly clear that money was going to be a problem. How much was a night out watching the football going to cost? Clare had hit the nail on the head though in one aspect, the people are ridiculously friendly. As well as highlighting the endearing character of the locals, the transaction also provided ample evidence of the need to get to grips with the nuances of the pronunciation of any Japanese words we attempted; two things exemplified the following morning when within seconds of looking slightly bewildered and weighed down by our bags in the same station, a man was at our side offering help.

"Can I help you find what you are looking for?" he asked in excellent English. *Good, this should be easy,* I thought.

"Thanks. We're trying to find where the Bullet Train leaves from."

"Where are you going?"

"Kyoto."

"Where?"

"Kyoto."

"Sorry, say it again."

"Kyoto."

"Can I see the ticket?"

"Ah . . . Kyoto," he declared in what appeared exactly the same tone. The gentleman, for that's what he was, didn't just point us off in the right direction though, he took us all the way through the turnstiles, found out what time the next train was leaving at, and from what platform. After all that I was a little upset that he neglected to wait with us for 20 minutes and then wave us off. It was hugely indicative of Japanese-English interaction, in fact there was to be a lot of trial and error in all aspects of our time in the country, but errors that instead of eliciting embarrassment only generated more perseverant help from the other side.

We returned to Tokyo two days later, after successfully finding our own way to the train on the other end. The friendly-man was not there to greet us, so we made our way out to the flat that we'd be renting for the next two nights. The United-Villa game was taking place later that day, and so as we were being escorted from the office to the flat, we asked about the finishing times – 12.30am – and consequently the start times – 5.30am – of the public transport. The Metro was our only method of getting home, and with the game not starting until 2.30am, it was going to be a long, and probably expensive night.

I knew even before going out for this game it was unlikely that I'd meet any United fans. It hadn't exactly proved a highly successful approach so far in Asia. The differences in culture and how that manifested itself in watching games was probably the biggest obstacle, but fans still went to stadiums, and Tokyo was a night-owl's paradise, so I guessed that there must be some common ground. It was with that in mind that I had decided a few days previously to go into the lion's den so to speak, and contact the Japanese branch of the Manchester United Supporters' Club, the very people that the club was pandering to in their attempts to secure a lasting fanbase in the country, and thus from my perspective, a group of people who could be considered the main culprits in perpetuating the ABU (Anyone But United) attitude in some quarters. My attempts to contact them met with stonewalled silence – perhaps a language issue was the problem, enthusiasm for the game shouldn't have been.

The country's appreciation of football, highlighted by the success of the J-League and the hosting of the 2002 World Cup, should have been more keenly developed than any of its Asian neighbours that I had visited thus far. Coupled with Japan's economic power, the reasons for United's interest here were obvious. The added advantage of the chance to play 'real' competitive matches in the country would also have helped develop a following. United have toured Japan in the past, in 2005 and 2007, but success in the Champions League finals of 1999 and 2008 had produced far more legitimate opportunities to visit in the form of the 1999 Intercontinental Cup and 2008 Club World Cup. Viewed with a dose of scepticism in the UK, it remains a FIFA obligation and certainly a step above summer friendlies in creating a genuine footballing atmosphere. The chance to see United play a full-strength side in a competitive match, and significantly lift a trophy (or in Giggs' case a giant key) would certainly have a longer lasting effect than any half-arsed kickabout. Missing out on the opportunity to compete in the 2009 edition after the Champions League final defeat in Rome, as it moves to its new location, the United Arab Emirates, is potentially a huge blow for any thoughts the club had of breaking new ground in the Middle East.

Japan has always felt like a different proposition though. The success of the J-League could initially provide impetus for a club like United, sparking interest in the big teams in the sport, but ultimately it should be a hindrance. The success of a nation's own league, the potential that gives for growing the game in the country, the advancement of the football family as Sepp Blatter often refers to, makes it a little bit of a mystery why FIFA's head never objects to these commercial tours where the big clubs come along and steal attention and focus from local sides (others such as Asia-chief Mohamed Bin Hamman have finally begun to). However, in Japan, it seems that above all else star-quality matters. Perhaps it replicates the individual nature of the sumo battle, but it is here more than anywhere that the tendency to follow a given player, rather than the team, rules.

Of those players, David Beckham was, and still is, the biggest. Totting-up shirt sales might not fully account for this as it is a general shift in recognition that follows him that is crucial. Beckham's importance to United commercially has often been overstated, but his impact in Japan is unparalleled and allowed the club to be confident enough that there was no need to try to replicate the Ji-Sung Park factor by chasing a Hidetoshi Nakata or Shunsuke Nakamura.

Any doubts over Beckham's notoriety in Japan are washed away by the results of an internet search using both Manchester United and Japan as keywords – the majority of hits are Beckham based. This was a country after all where in 2003 they produced a three-metre-high chocolate figure of him, and he became the only footballer to the best of my knowledge to go on a promotional tour purely to promote himself; a jaunt fully paid for by Castrol Oil, lasting just four days but thought to have nearly matched his entire first season's salary at Madrid.

It was significant that Beckham's tour came hot on the heels of that move to Real Madrid, thus just as he broke free of tough rules imposed by United to prevent players fully exploiting their commercial value (just one of the reported motivations in Cristiano Ronaldo's desire to leave, after he was said to be annoyed at allowing an option with GE Finance to lapse). In Japan Beckham has been the face of everything from mobile phones to beauty ranges, while 'Bekkamu', the name by which he is know in the country, achieved a startling 90 per cent hit recognition amongst citizens. This is a staggering figure for a foreigner, considering that judges in the UK have failed to recognise both Gazza and the Spice Girls at the peak of their respective fames.

Beckham of course is a law unto himself, ever keen to impress with pedantic attention to every positive PR detail – small wonder the Samurai haircut he sported on that 2003 tour – but he undoubtedly helped the club's ambitions. United could, for instance, probably be confident that Beckham's captain's role in England's participation in the 2002 World Cup was enough brand-strengthening for one year, and perhaps was behind their decision to skip Asia in 2003 in favour of the US. But does this actually make Japan the most difficult of all Asian countries, surely a country that respects star quality to such a degree is inevitably the most fickle? Could United ever really be confident of declaring a student from Osaka a United fan, when he might just hang on the every move of Wayne Rooney? Would their rumoured under-26 with re-sale value transfer policy, with the onus on developing stars to sell on, not only damage their standing in Japan, but in fact consistently hand the advantage to their rivals that inevitably purchase these players from them? Is their endorse-ment-block preventing players from fully exploiting their commercial value not actively disadvantageous to their goals in Japan? More impor-tantly to me, did the 'star-craze' kick really come from watching a league game against Villa at 2.30am on a Saturday night, or only from the mega-hyped clashes of a 'Grand Slam Sunday' or simply the pages of the gossip sheets?

It was going to be an all-nighter, that much was already established, so with a lack of eagerness to leave we hung around flicking between the two television channels available to us. Our flat seemed to occupy an alterna-tive reality to the high-tech, uber-chic modernity of the Tokyo of adver-tising campaigns, in every aspect that is aside from its compactness. One of the channels was carrying the November Grand Sumo Tournament, an event that we had been hoping to go and watch, but its location in Fukoka down in the south of the country had made, as you can guess, the travelling costs prohibitive.

Predictably Sumo is a distinctively Japanese pursuit bursting with tradition and ceremony with similarities to football (a worrying rise in foreign wrestlers in some stables was halted by the introduction of a 'cap'), yet wholly idiosyncratic demands (sumo wrestlers are not allowed to drive cars, a rule introduced following an accident involving a wrestler). As a live event it might be quite dramatic, but on television it certainly wasn't making me regret missing it too much. They were part way through an 18-day event that was supposedly part of a national obsession, yet there was no palpable evidence of the tournament's existence outside the confines of our flat – where it would have been interesting just to try to get a wrestler to fit. A similar event at home would surely be noticeable nationwide, imagine the sights and sounds of Wimbledon for instance, yet this seemed to pass under the radar. In such circumstances I doubted how much outwardly noticeable appreciation of a football match taking place in England there'd be.

Around 10pm, we decided to make our way to Roppongi, the area popular with night-owls and westerners, because of its proximity to the financial district and many embassies. The area was dripping with bars and via a quick trip off the beaten track to discover the Sports Café where we were going to watch the game, we returned to the main thoroughfare that was buzzing with bright lights. It was like the hyperactive younger brother of Kyoto, a place more akin to the 'traditional' Japanese ceremony of the sumo, awash as it was with temples. The Roppongi scene was not quite as authentic as you'd perhaps want though, as westerners and Japanese milled around in almost equal numbers and tourists became the cannon fodder for bar promoters offering cheap drinks and free entry.

After sampling three or four bars we made our way to the Sports Café at about 1am, with 90 minutes remaining before the 90 minutes I was there for. The general destruction of all my best-laid budgeting plans continued apace with the £14 each it cost just to get in, although we did receive a free drink for that. Yippee. There were screens up showing the earlier games, and with one particularly big one in the corner, we headed over after claiming our free drink. At £7 for a bottle of Corona we basically had no choice but to say 'sod it, let's try not to worry about the money' – something it appeared Clare had already done as recompense for having to spend her Saturday night in Tokyo in such a way. The spiralling cost also had the unfortunate side-effect of preventing me from questioning any pointless purchases she made for the entirety of the trip from that point, with 'remember the Tokyo football night' becoming a catchphrase of sorts.

Watching the game itself became almost a distraction from the events going on around us. The place was carnage as a Saturday night got into full swing with alcohol flowing freely in all corners. It was a unique clientele for a sports bar that was for sure, and the photo bedecked walls featuring celebrities from Ben Affleck to Hugh Grant to Rio Ferdinand all with the owner, proved it was more celeb haunt than gritty football pub.

Back home Clare and I have a basic trade-off between football and a combination of *Coronation Street* and whatever version, cycle or nation that happens to be searching for its 'next top-model' at any given point. The result of which is that while much to her chagrin Clare can freely tell you why the 'squeaky bum time' quote attributed to Fergie is incorrect or freely recall the names of the Premier League's 20 managers, I can confidently tell you that being 'fierce' is a prerequisite for a successful model in Tyra Banks' self-important world and that Miss Jay is a run-way diva extraordinaire. And so it was that from where we were sat on a long seat facing the big-screen in the corner, I could positively identify that the group of women that was oscillating between five and ten were participants in some incarnation of *America's Next Top Model*.

Whilst I sat and tried to watch the football, Clare gave an incisive run-down on the ins and outs of the fully formed cliques that were 'performing' before us, and ultimately identified who might win the show. It was dramatic stuff – one of the would-be models was clearly becoming isolated from the rest of the group, so she wasn't going to win, and lived up to expectations by breaking down in tears. As the first half progressed they were becoming ever more fidgety, constantly standing up, and with their freakishly tall and spindly frames were starting to block the screen. They weren't speaking English, I was guessing German, but I was getting to the point of asking them to move; thinking whilst readying myself to kick up a fuss that this trip was really fleshing out my character – not only was I becoming obsessed by the price of everything, spending about ten per cent of everyday merely calculating our daily budget over and over, I was now also a train aficionado (or was it railway enthusiast?) of sorts and was about to top that by asking ten models to move out of the way of the television on a Saturday night so that I could watch football. Well I didn't actually ask. Instead of saying: 'Look would you mind moving your giant gangly bodies out the way and stop wielding your comparatively large heads in all directions because you're preventing me from watching men in shorts run around in the rain in the Midlands,' I went for some pretty angry hand gestures, and a few noises that were lost in the music. They got the picture though, and sat down for a few minutes. Yes indeed, they knew they were in the wrong.

By half-time the group had fractured and the 'model' who was being shirked had finished her little cry and was sitting on her own. A couple of the others returned to give her a pep talk, and eventually she left with them.

Clare loved every second of it, and wanted to find out more, although her attempts to persuade me to go and ask them if they were really off TV wasn't going anywhere. My simple and rather effective argument was based on my objection to going up to someone in a bar and asking: 'are you a model?' So Clare did it instead. She was already in a sports bar watching football and drinking beer on a Saturday night, so why not try and complete a transition to alpha-male and go and use a cheesy chat-up line whilst slurringly drunk. It turned out that they were models in a television competition, and it seems to have been *Switzerland's Next Top Model*.

With the entertainment seemingly over the focus shifted to the second half, albeit momentarily. The hotseat was taken by just two people but it appeared we were to be treated to another show. A western businessman, probably in his late forties, was accompanied by a young lady who, you didn't need to be Hercule Poirot to realise, was not his wife. Admittedly the conversation between the two was not exactly flowing, but this was not the by-product of a contemptuous relationship borne out of years of familiarity, it was rather because there was no evident connection between them aside from the potential his wallet held to meet the additional clothing costs that would enable her to cover the remainder of her body in fabric.

Champagne on ice soon arrived, although he was clearly not interested in a drink, that was just another prop in the show.

"Par for the course 'round here," a 50-or-so-year-old English guy called Paul who worked in Tokyo's financial sector, and whom I'd chatted to briefly at half-time, proffered. He was the only other person watching the match.

"Yeah?"

"Yep, strippers, always coming here," he added, perhaps a little too knowingly. "I'd like to see him try and explain that bottle of champagne on the account to his wife."

We were clearly not the only ones who thought it was an awkward scene however – and luckily the position of the big screen was enabling us to digest every second – the stripper's attempts to fire up conversation were floundering in one word exchanges, so she decided to revert to her tried and trusted A-game, a la footballer in a penalty shoot-out. She shuffled slightly closer to her companion, ran her fingers through her long blonde hair, and began whipping him with her ponytail. Clare and I burst out laughing. They glared at us, but my pointing to the screen had them convinced they were not the object of hilarity and the whipping continued. Eight, nine, ten, eleven lashes were completed before the man dressed in a Marks and Spencer's jumper put his hand up to bring it to a halt . . . in order to fish a stray hair out of his mouth.

They only stayed for another ten minutes, plenty long enough for one more quick bout of hair whipping, but they left with barely a sip taken from their champagne. It seemed an excellent opportunity to see out the rest of the game with a couple of glasses of bubbly rather than spend another fortune on beer. So under the guise of a trip to the toilet, I grabbed the glasses (without really wondering who was going to drink from the glass the stripper had been using) plonked them on the table and went to the bathroom. By the time I came back the whole bucket was there.

"Where did this come from?"

"Well, Paul reckoned we should go for the whole lot." *Fair enough*, I thought, but that proved our undoing. The staff were obviously attracted by our sudden affluence and came across to rather pedantically take it away – in fact they even poured the champagne from the glasses back into the bottle – what was the point of that? It'd already been paid for and they couldn't reserve it. Paul obviously thought so too, and knowing the manager shot-off to speak to him, promising to get it back for us. He returned shortly afterwards tail between his legs. Apparently at $600 per bottle they hadn't been that keen to hand it back over.

I didn't fully understand why Paul was there at all. He had recently, he said, allowed his subscription to the correct combination of SKY channels to lapse but he didn't support either United or Villa. He told us that there were a number of similar sports bars in the city, but that they were generally filled with Americans, so he often came here. That didn't surprise me, Japanese people had generally been pleasantly surprised to find we were not just more Americans, delighted that other nationalities were visiting, a promising sign ahead of Tokyo's 2016 Olympic bid. Paul also reckoned the bar would be full come next Wednesday night/Thursday morning, when the United v Villarreal Champions League group stage game kicked-off. I was not as sure, it was emptying now shortly before 4am, and so in the middle of the week at 6.30am? It seemed unlikely.

The match came to an end shortly before 4.30am, leaving another hour or so before the metro started up again and we'd already spent somewhere in the region of £130 on the night. This was more expensive than going to the game itself – and in the end I opted to use the computer in the communal area of the hostel to take advantage of UEFA's online streaming for Wednesday night's match. It was worth it too, as a 4.45am kick-off meant that for the first time I was getting up to watch the game rather than trying to stay awake for it. Japan was in a funny time-zone for the regular viewer. Some games you'd probably stay up for, others grab an early night to rise before the larks, and in my case shortly before a heavy-set and ponytailed Englishman got up to smash his feet on pavement and lift paving slabs to help secure a future in sumo.

Following the Aston Villa game we finally rolled in at 6.45am, after a great night out. This was the first time I'd thought that we'd had a great night out because of the football. It was the football's 'fault' that we'd been there, that we'd stayed so long, and yes Clare, that we'd spent so much. But it was the first sign football was actually enriching the adventure, not hindering it. The following day we managed nothing, partly due to a killer hangover and in part because we were conserving our energy for the next day's trip into quintessential Japan. We'd ummed and ahhed but we were going to rise exceptionally early to make at least the tail end of the auction at the Tsukiji sashimi market, and eat the freshest of fresh sushi. Given the location of our flat and the time the metro started, we figured that if we left at 5am, we'd be there at 6, to catch the closing stages of what is generally perceived as Tokyo's tourist highlight. Having proudly resisted the temptation to hit the off button on the alarm our delight and self-satisfaction grew as we sat on the empty Metro, proving how hardcore we had become; no-one else was really going this early. All-nighter one day, 4am rise the next. Sleep: I spit on you.

Once off the metro the stench of fish led us in the right direction, but the action seemed minimal, surely we hadn't missed the whole event? We rounded the corner and saw two clueless Americans consulting their guidebook. Shit. Something was amiss. It turned out to be a Japanese public holiday and so the whole thing was shut down for the day. That's Japan for you.

India

AT 9.20PM ON Wednesday 26 November, gunmen began a series of coordinated attacks at key tourist landmarks in the city of Mumbai that lasted for three days. As the attacks began we slept in Tokyo. Our flight to India was booked for early morning on Thursday 27 November, initially taking us to Sri Lanka, with a six-hour layover, for which we were planning to stay in the airport. By coincidence our search for information on safaris the previous day had led to us re-confirming our flight in an STA Travel office in Tokyo. I'd never bothered to re-confirm a flight before, and so we were lucky to find out that the Sri Lanka–India leg had actually been cancelled and we'd need to stay in Colombo, Sri Lanka's capital, for a day.

It wasn't until we arrived at Tokyo's Narita airport early on the morning of the 27th that we learnt of the attacks. After seeing images on a television screen, we found an internet café to fill in the blanks. It was clearly an on-going situation that was sending India, and Mumbai in particular, into a frenzied state, but details were shaky, and the depth of the crisis was still unclear. We were committed to the flight, having already checked in, and as we had the day's wait in Sri Lanka, we decided to keep up-to-date with the information and continue as planned.

We arrived in Colombo at about two in the morning and were driven to the accommodation we'd managed to book. It was an enlightening drive. Having only a cursory knowledge of the fragile situation in the country (before things worsened in early 2009) I was of the belief that the problems between the government and the separatist seeking Tamils were restricted to the north of the country, so to be stopped twice by military personnel armed with machine guns on the 40-minute drive from airport to hotel was unnerving. On both occasions we were required to leave the car and show our passports while the vehicle was searched. Sure, the soldiers were some of the politest people I'd ever met, but coming completely unexpectedly, and still being punch drunk from a long flight, it was a little hard to digest. Our driver nonchalantly told us it was a day of national celebration, so security was even tighter. When we told him we were flying to India, he just laughed and said, "be careful."

Our stayover in Sri Lanka was around 22 hours, and by the time we awoke there were about 15 left. Almost every television channel carried a constant news barrage from India. The situation was, if anything, spiralling out of control. Certainly no resolution seemed imminent. The British Foreign Office was advising against all travel to Mumbai and surrounding areas. The city, formerly known as Bombay, had been one of the intended stops on our Indian sojourn. I had a contact there too, a United fan, who was going to show us around. In a country that was most definitely Clare's choice, Mumbai was the city I most wanted to visit.

It's very easy to say: 'Oh well, India's a big place. What's the problem? Something has already happened, it's not going to happen again.' But when the Foreign Office questions travelling somewhere and you are about to fly there, although really you don't *have* to go, it's a very different story. Yes, things could pass off without problem, there are risks in a lot of countries, but in the face of advice to the contrary, you have to decide whether it is really worth taking the chance.

We felt as though we were just being wimps, after all I had moved to London about three days after the 7 July attacks in 2005, and hadn't had a second thought about it, while Clare already lived there. But something felt different about this terrorist situation. We didn't really know anything about the country at ground level, which robbed us of a natural instinct to make the correct decisions about what is, and what isn't right, plus this was an on-going situation. What if it escalated? This terrorism just felt more dangerous. There had been over 400 people killed in bombings in incidents in major cities in India since 2005. In September 2008 there had been two separate bombing incidents in just two weeks in the capital, New Delhi.

We were unsure what to do. We considered flying directly to Africa to go on safari, which was to be the next leg of our journey. It was hard to make a decision that wasn't financially dictated, but we decided, after consulting STA who were busy refunding all Mumbai travel and other Indian flight tickets, to go ahead. We were flying initially to Cochin in the south, with the intention to travel next to Goa and then on to Mumbai. That seemed unlikely now, but we'd see how things panned out. I seriously doubted we'd be sticking to our original plans, and fired off an email to my contact, Rahul, to see how things were from his point of view. Going from my most eagerly anticipated destination to my least was bad enough as it was, now things could be a lot worse. We watched the news for the whole day wondering whether we had made a wise decision.

FORT KOCHI

Manchester City (a) 1-0
UK time: 30/11/08, 13.30
Local time: 30/11/08, 19.00

We landed in Kerala, a communist state in the south-west of India. The self-proclaimed 'God's Own Country' was where we'd be for the next game; the small matter of the Manchester derby. After whizzing through the surprisingly slack security and immigration procedures on both ends of the flight, we got in a taxi for our transfer to Fort Kochi (one of three urban districts comprising Cochin) where we'd be staying.

Living up to the expectation that stepping out into India is like stepping into an oven, it was stiflingly hot. Our month's acclimatisation in south-east Asia didn't seem to have prepared us in the least for this and we spent much of the car journey with our heads out of the windows like dogs, trying to inhale something that didn't just feel warm, as a multitude of intense colours and noises flashed by. Japan had been different – with complications of language and alien nuances of culture, but a lot of its big city architecture and quality infrastructure felt familiar to our western sensitivities. India, however, seemed instantly out of the ordinary. The brightness was the most striking thing, the strength of that sunlight igniting the medley of colour reverberating from dress, architecture and even highly decorated trucks that careered down the road. It felt as though life up to now had been in black and white, and that plain old colour had been skipped entirely by a direct jump to high definition.

Fort Kochi was not a heaving metropolis by any means, instead a small seaside town popular with foreigners landing in Cochin. It was a relaxing initiation into Indian life and seemed a world away from the troubles of Mumbai. Some notoriety was being garnered from hosting the Indian stop-over of the 'Volvo Ocean Race 2008-2009' the week immediately following our visit. In general however, it was more famed for its Basilica, its Chinese fishing nets and the opportunity to see Kathakali dances. In short it was a small and relatively remote place – the football could be a problem. This might be the biggest test yet of United's global appeal.

The Chinese fishing nets and Kathakali dance immediately revealed the nature of what was to become my relationship with India; the juxtaposition of the remarkably good and incredibly annoying, pretentious and over-hyped. The Chinese fishing nets, which helped make up for our farcically failed trip to the Tsukiji sashimi market in Tokyo, are situated right on the water, lifting fresh fish directly onto the beach where you can buy pretty much anything from crab and lobster to the biggest tiger prawns you've ever seen, to fish such as red snapper. You can then walk about 100 yards with your prize and have it cooked at a stall in butter and lemon. We opted for prawns and snapper, choosing our purchase point based on the friendliness of the guy, and the fact that he wore the iconic West German national shirt of Italia 90. Iconic to me certainly, representing the wonder of the first World Cup I fully invested my time in at the age of 11. Absorbing every minute I could, every second I was allowed to stay up for, revelling in a tournament ridiculously touted as the nadir of the world game.

Before England met them in the semi-final and I was being told to hate them at every turn, Germany, with the power of Lothar Matthaus and the perfect forward partnership of Jurgen Klinsmann and Rudi Voller were my 'other' team, but then I wasn't viewing the whole thing as an extension of the war as the English media love to do. Why a man in India was celebrating this team as well was a mystery. Voller had been my favourite, perhaps his too? Hold on, wasn't there some sort of six degrees of separation thing going on here? Man in Germany shirt selling fish to Chinese fishing nets to Chinese spitting to Rudi Voller to Voller and Frank Rijkaard spitting to Italia 90 World Cup to man in Germany shirt selling fish from Chinese fishing nets. Maybe the spread of football worldwide is merely down to spitting; the evidence was clearly stacking up. Anyway, it all made for the freshest meal (no phlegm) I've ever eaten, needless to say for a fraction of the price of back home. My only complaint was a bird crapping on my shoulder halfway through – but that's lucky right?

Kathakali performance on the other hand was, to summarise, downright bloody awful. It is a dance-drama characterised by expressive make-up, where the actors use eye and body movement in-tune with accompanying percussion to convey meaning. The most interesting bit is watching them mix and apply their own extensive make-up, which they do on the stage, before 'the real drama' gets underway. I found it to be a terrible experience, but the woman next to me was the perfect example of the people I feared meeting in India. Those travellers who are seeking to 'find themselves', and approach everything as though it is the best thing they've ever seen (obviously oblivious to Lee Sharpe's back-heel against Barcelona or Mark Hughes' volley against Oldham in the 1994 FA Cup semi-final) in the painful attempt to prove they are spiritually connected with another culture or have a higher calling. One result is the distinct lack of a quality filter and blind loyalty to everything and anything they see. She was practically gushing, and happy to tell anyone who would listen how fantastic, how amazing it was, and so "full of expression". I felt lucky; 'finding myself' wasn't on the agenda. I already knew where I was. I was in India, wasting two-and-a-half hours shifting in my front-row seat while watching a chap in green make-up pull the same face over and over again. It made me pine for the joys of Wimbledon away back in the Crazy Gang days. I was more than happy to immerse myself in another culture (the one involving John Fashanu and Sam Hammam often proved more interesting than this), and explore the new experiences waiting for me, but that wasn't going to come without an ounce of cynicism.

The air conditioning proved a blessed relief. We were staying in a 'home-stay' rather than a hostel or hotel. It was dirt cheap, but didn't really do what it said on the tin. We had been promised some air-con in our room and an ample social area with a television. The room was sweat-inducing to say the least, and I regularly woke up during our stay there with wet hair, and was consequently 'enjoying' three showers a day. One other room, of the three, was filled. It had the television and the air-conditioning, and a couple in their fifties, who were busy 'finding themselves'. Now Kochi was nice, but they'd stayed there for six months (we covered it readily enough in three days). In six months they'd have time to lose and find themselves any number of times.

This couple were busy filling us in on all this in the less than ample social area on the evening of the City game. My attempts to find some-where to watch the match had proved predictably unfulfilling; there was simply nowhere in Fort Kochi that would show it. As it was, alcohol licences were thin on the ground, leaving most people drinking their 'special tea' from teapots, and anyway the nightly powercut would hit just after kick-off time (it was scheduled you see; changing times every fortnight) so there was no chance of a sports bar. We'd potentially found a location in Ernakulum, a 20-minute boat ride away in an expensive hotel, but getting back would be problematic as the ferries between the two locations shut down around 9pm, and the game was not kicking-off until 7pm. In the vain hope that there was another option I'd overlooked, the previous night I'd asked Benson, the convivial host and owner of the homestay, if he'd any ideas. He'd thought about it for a while before telling me that he might be able to persuade our fellow guests to let us have the television out in the communal area for the evening. Texting him on the day elicited no reply, and so we were close to resigning ourselves to an awkward trip home from another island, before Benson turned up around 5.30pm. With the other two in the room with us it was difficult to crowbar the question in, but having asked Benson if, "there was any luck with the television?" he was proud to announce, "yeah, yeah, it's absolutely fine. You're watching it at my house with me." Cool, he even had a back-up generator to get us through the power cut.

In the meantime, Benson's wife had turned up to cook a little bit of food for the long-stayers, and he insisted that Clare and I also tried a bit. The English woman who was so keen to find herself, dressed in full Indian garb, was a little put out by the whole event, even saying: "Oh, you normally have to be here for at least six weeks before you get to try any food."

"Oh, do you?" I replied.

"They're going to Benson's house later," her husband added.

"What for?"

"They're coming to watch football with me. And drink," Benson said, slipping a bottle of vodka from his pocket. The woman's face was a picture of incredulity. Serves you right for stealing all the air-conditioning, which come to think of it is hardly a part of authentic Indian life anyway. Ashamed though I am to admit it, quite probably a smug smile crept onto my face, but her bitterness came flooding out for the next five minutes and she even resorted to trotting out the old: 'Oh, Manchester City fans are actually from Manchester' line. Sorry, but football opens doors. United had opened this door.

Despite the offer of Benson's vodka we felt that we should provide our own beer for the evening and so enquired if there was anywhere we, minus a teapot, could go and buy booze. He directed us to a 'wine shop' ten minutes' walk away. Despite relatively strict alcohol laws, including an outright ban on alcohol advertising, Kerala's per capita liquor consumption rate (at 8.3 litres) is the highest in India and three times higher than the national average. We arrived at the 'wine shop' and were presented with something a little different to Oddbins. A queue of men stood lined-up against a wall, taking it in turns to stand in front of a cage that housed the alcohol, to make their purchase. Upon our arrival we were ushered forward immediately, completely bypassing the queues, to reach the mesh – this, I cynically assumed, meant we were about to be ripped off. However, it seems that as the wine shops are all state owned, there is also a state-enforced retail price for the beers that is printed on the bottle and strictly adhered to. So away we walked with a box full of giant bottles of Kingfisher. Perfect match-watching fare.

When we returned, Benson was not quite ready to go, but could see I was getting rather anxious to get over to his house and get watching. So, making sure our beer was hidden from public view, another alcohol restriction (the bottle we'd already opened was stashed in Clare's bag), he dispatched his son Donovan, who was probably about 11, to lead us across the road to the family home, where he'd be joining us in a few minutes. We respectfully removed our shoes and made our way into the lounge. There was a resounding crack as we passed through the door and six necks snapped towards us. This could be awkward. No wonder Benson spent his time hanging out across the road if this was what his house was like. Two other children, aside from Donovan, a grandfather and a grandmother all stared at us.

"Hello," we said.

"Hello," everyone replied, as we stood there, Clare clutching an open bottle of beer, and me with a box of the stuff.

"ESPN," Donovan said, and chased his brother to retrieve the remote. It was bad, they had all been watching some sort of television game show together.

"Cricket?" one of the smaller children asked.

"No, football . . . Manchester," Donovan replied, as we stood in the doorway, gormless smiles on our faces. Granddad Benson spoke to the children, and then pointed towards a wicker sofa.

"Sit, sit," he said. Donovan flicked the channel over.

"Yes, that looks like it. Thank you," I added. Grandmother Benson got up and went into the kitchen. Uh-oh, we'd driven one of them out already.

"Ok, this is awkward," Clare whispered to me. "Get a beer out."

"No way. This is bad enough."

"Look I have a beer in my hand, you get one out too."

"Really?"

"Do it."

The game was kicking-off, but everyone was still looking at us. This is where it got really difficult. There was clearly a strict set of rules regarding alcohol, so this was going to be a delicate situation. Benson seemed to pop over to the home-stay on a regular basis to enjoy a drink with his guests. Did that mean that he didn't like people drinking in his house? No, couldn't do, he'd sent us over with the beer. True. But normally I'd offer a beer to Granddad Benson, but if he was not of the alcohol ilk then would that offend him? Maybe? Trying to reach a sensible middle ground between making sure we didn't offend them, and just sitting clutching a box of beer all to our selves was proving extremely problematic – it was driving me to paranoia.

"Get a beer," Clare nudged me.

"Ok. Should I offer one?"

"I don't know."

I reached tentatively towards the box, now at my feet. "Glass," Granddad Benson called immediately.

"Yes, please. You?" I countered, slipping the question in almost inaudibly. He shook his head, and spoke quickly in what I presumed was Malayalam, the most prominent language in the state, to Donovan, who was despatched to the kitchen for two glasses. He returned and slumped back into his seat. The only problem now was that the bottles weren't open. Out of politeness, I didn't want to ask immediately, so, whilst Clare poured hers from the already open bottle, I hesitated. Granddad Benson soon despatched Donovan to the kitchen again, this time to retrieve a bottle opener. He slumped back into his seat, whilst his two brothers chatted away to each other. It was clear that whatever burden of responsibility there was to be borne by the children in the family, as the oldest, Donovan was the one to bear it.

The game had begun and Granddad Benson was finally facing the television instead of us. He'd actually brought himself another chair and moved much closer to the set. Donovan and his nearest sibling were sitting relatively still watching the game, as was I. Things were now more settled, allowing me time to fully take in the surroundings. The room was deep set, with small windows, presumably to prevent easy access for the scorching sun. The walls were lined with settees and other chairs were stacked nearby for easy access, telling its own story of a revolving door of guests. The only other furniture was at the far end where the television sat on a large wooden unit below a wall-hanging – the only item you'd have immediately considered traditionally Indian. Granddad Benson was wearing a Lungi (the traditional clothing worn by men in Kerala, a sheet of cloth designed for easy access for air, that can be folded into something that closely resembles a nappy) and all the women were dressed as extravagantly as you'd expect, but it was the constant flow of people that made the home most unique. That 'settled' state was short-lived.

Clare – the biggest of the children, with seemingly the shortest attention span – was soon involved in a game with the youngest child, Ruben, that involved holding a teddy bear, allowing him to run towards it and then throwing it over his head. It was a little like playing with a dog with the general repetitiveness of the movement. I took the opportunity to try and keep the focus on football, asking Donovan and his brother, who were at least sat still, if they liked the sport.

"Yes," was their resounding reply.

"And which team do you like?"

"Your team is Manchester?" Donovan countered.

"Yes United – the team in red."

"My team is also Manchester United," Donovan added to the general approval of his brother. They were aligning their support with their guest's. "Although Manchester City is sometimes good, so is Arsenal," he added. Hmm, maybe not so much then. His brother clearly didn't agree though and booed him.

"And which players do you know from Manchester United and the Premier League?" This set off a clamour of answers as the pair raced to name Rooney and Ronaldo quickest. The younger brother, whose name was never actually revealed at any point (he was only ever described as the 'Smaller One') took the honours as the most enthusiastic. Clearly Premier League, and United heroes in particular, had infiltrated southern India.

"Ferdinand." That was Granddad Benson joining in, but not turning around; he was transfixed by the action. The Rooney/Ronaldo screaming race had led to the Smaller One jumping to his feet, and attempting to get involved in the game of bear retrieval. He now stood on the other end of Clare's throws, partially blocking my view of the television whilst retrieving and throwing the toy back to her as Ruben shuttled back and forth between the two. This now continued until he started crying, at which point Granddad Benson would raise an eyebrow and the toy would be returned. The monotonous game re-started every minute or so, spasmodically bringing Grandmother Benson back from the kitchen to admonish Smaller One, sending him scuttling to his seat but only delaying proceedings momentarily.

Benson's wife soon added to the numbers, returning from across the road and dampening her sons' over active spirits for a short time. Smaller One joined Donovan on the sofa who was trying his hardest to retain an air of maturity and concentration by glaring at the television. It was all quiet until another slightly more famous errant child caused mayhem; Wayne Rooney hit a 42nd minute goal. I cheered a little (I'd been trying to restrict my reactions and keep them to a minimum throughout), but Donovan and the Smaller One ran to the television cheering and diving on top of each other. I felt safe enough to get to my feet in appreciation as Granddad Benson clapped, smiled and turned to me, "Your team? Your team?"

"Yes, indeed." Had he not thought that all along?

Grandmother Benson was quickly to the doorway at the noise, but seeing me on my feet as well, soon figured out what had happened and returned to the peace and quiet of the kitchen. The goal had sparked some real jubilation in this tiny corner of the world, or perhaps more likely, had just given kids with plenty of steam to let off a legitimate reason to make noise and escape a telling-off.

At half-time, the teddy-throwing began again (certainly a more interesting half-time diversion than a penalty shoot-out. Old Trafford please take note, perhaps a Lou Macari throwing for the new season?) and then Benson eventually showed up putting a stop to all things mischievous. As soon as he came through the door it was noticeable that with barely a word Donovan and the Smaller One sat down, a sign of paternal discipline if ever there was one, with Ruben the only one ignoring him. It turned out Ruben wasn't actually part of the family and was from another down the road. They'd left him there for the weekend, and he was apparently a bit unsure about what was going on.

Benson's half-time appearance naturally led to a discussion of the game, and I found his knowledge of football was restricted mainly to English national team players, key amongst them Peter Shilton, Gary Lineker and Paul Gascoigne, with later knowledge of another striker, who after some guess work turned out to be Alan Shearer. It seemed as though Italia 90 had been more popular in Fort Kochi than anywhere else. He said that it was in fact the Smaller One (his words) that preferred football, and actually played, and that Donavan was more interested in cricket – you could have fooled me. Benson himself had pleasingly only heard of United, Chelsea and Arsenal, and not Liverpool. A clear sign that Premier League success was dictating popularity? He no longer had the time to watch, thus evidence that it was trophy-winning clubs that had achieved recognition with the general public in Kerala. However, his comment that cricket was now making big inroads into football's popularity in India was surprising. I naturally thought it was the other way around. India was supposed to be the next big football market, and the next big economy. Surely cricket had been established for years? But apparently some consider Kerala's major sport to be football. This conversation left me confused as to the status of the two sports in the country.

Benson was soon on his way, as he said "too busy for the football" – after all he had vodka to sup with his procession of friends across the road. As the second half kicked-off, suddenly the hired help appeared from the kitchen and plonked some samosas down in front us. Where did she come from? Obviously we ate them, aside from the one Ruben picked up and licked before putting back down. What great hospitality.

I watched football, Granddad Benson watched football, but the others continued 'playing'. Grandmother Benson appeared again like an apparition, and Clare, realising that things were getting out of hand, ended her involvement in the teddy game, particularly as I'd just had to tell Ruben not to smack her on the head with an old torch. In fairness he actually listened to me, and put the torch back where it had come from.

Smaller One was growing evermore frustrated by Ruben, who didn't seem the brightest button in the box and continued to wreak havoc. In frustration, Smaller One, who was now being wound up by Donovan too but who'd up to then not really done much wrong, struck out at Ruben. Almost before the guest child had opened his mouth to cry, Grandmother Benson stormed out from the kitchen, with a large raffia stick in hand, and struck Smaller One. If things had been uncomfortable before it had just got a whole lot worse. The kid was screaming in agony, and she smacked him about five or six times before she retreated to the kitchen. Deathly silence filled the room, and the last 20 minutes of the game were watched in an uncomfortably low-key atmosphere, only broken by Smaller One's wailing.

About five minutes from full-time, two more adults, who were evidently Ruben's parents such was the child's delight at seeing them, appeared. Seeing Smaller One upset they went into the kitchen after exchanging pleasantries with us, and began a heated discussion, we presumed, over the caning that had been dished out in front of their son. It was somewhat of a relief when the full-time whistle went. Despite the 1-0 win, it hadn't quite been the enjoyable experience I'd hoped for. The hospitality we'd been shown was overwhelmingly generous – I certainly wouldn't have allowed two strangers to watch football in my house, let alone shape my family's evening around it and on top of that provide snacks. But it was hard to ignore the caning. We jumped to our feet and I tried to hide my delight over the victory in the circumstances, but Granddad Benson was at it again: "You win? Your team?!"

"Yes Granddad Benson." Come on it's not that complicated, really.

To try to relieve the pressure a bit, and to show how appreciative we really were, I got our camera out to take a picture. Everyone rumbled out into the lounge, including a few people we hadn't yet seen, to pose for the picture. Smaller One even cracked a smile. Benson met us halfway across the road on our way back, and all he wanted to know was when the next game was, and if we could watch it in his house. We'd be gone by then, in fact on another boat, we told him, a houseboat in the backwaters of Alleppey, potentially missing a Carling Cup tie with Blackburn and he seemed genuinely disappointed. To finish the night, Benson directed us down the road to the only restaurant he thought would be open, and we had the last thing on their menu, a tomato fry. I hate tomatoes, but I liked this. India was strange.

KOVALAM
Sunderland (h) 1-0
UK time: 06/12/08, 17.30
Local time: 06/12/08, 23.00

Aalborg (h) 2-2
UK time: 10/12/08, 19.45
Local time: 11/12/08, 01.45

Tottenham (a) 0-0
UK time: 13/12/08, 17.30
Local time: 13/12/08, 23.00

OUR overnight houseboat trip on the backwaters of Alleppey was one of the highlights of our entire trip and it proved a couple of things. Firstly that the tiger prawns that we ate in Fort Kochi weren't the biggest you could find, as they were trumped by a fisherman who rowed right up to our houseboat; and secondly that India remains a country whose compelling landscape is never done justice on film. It was the most expensive thing that we did for our entire time in India, but certainly the best. United's Carling Cup quarter-final was taking place on the other side of the planet on that particular night, but I'd already resigned myself to missing it. Unless of course there was a television on the boat.

There was. And it was huge. But in this case its only purpose was vanity, allowing our captain to show us a DVD of his part in the Alleppey snakeboat race victory back in 2006. That was to be my sporting quota for the night, the television not being connected to any form of reception, and besides we discovered the game wasn't being broadcast anyway.

While we'd grown used to making up our plans as we went along, we'd always at least had an idea in which direction we were travelling. The terror attacks had changed that, forcing us to scrap our initial plan to head immediately north through Goa and Mumbai on the way to a brief stop in Delhi before hitting Agra and Rajasthan. Mumbai was still a no-go area as far as the Foreign Office was concerned and thus an unnecessary risk at this stage, so we decided that splitting the country in two was the best option; half the time in the south and half the time in the north. As a replacement for the beach life of Goa we'd decided to lower our travelling principles considerably and head for a week's stop in Kovalam, a regular target for European package holiday makers.

Our initial five-day stay grew to eight when with a safari in Africa sorted we knew we had two months, rather than four weeks, in India. This meant that our time in Kovalam would easily be our longest in any place so far, and that would span three United games. However, what had been blazingly apparent so far in India was the lack of anywhere at all to watch football in public, so I hoped that a tourist resort, more aware of the desires of the European visitor, might have the bars and cable channels I needed. As a back-up we made sure we had a room with a television.

Good job really. Nice beachfront locations matter little in the absence of televisions and in the face of prohibitive licensing laws preventing bars from staying open late enough to show the games even if correctly equipped. So it was that I watched three consecutive matches in the confines of our room. The opening game against Sunderland saw me fall asleep during a game for the first time on the trip, a record I'd been proud of up to then, waking as the replays of United's goal were running, while the Spurs match in the same time slot the following Saturday was the nadir of my first travelling illness, and I certainly wasn't going to be leaving the room that day anyway.

The midweek European game against Aalborg, sandwiched between these two fairly humdrum league matches, introduced me to a new channel: Ten Sports. Unfortunately they'd chosen to broadcast the Arsenal match that still had something riding on it and show the United game on a replay starting at 3.15am. Turned out I'd found my breaking point. I wasn't going to stay up till 5am for the full-time whistle in a replay. There was a replay of the replay at 2pm the following day and that was just going to have to be good enough. With that decided, I engineered a low-key rendition of the infamous *Likely Lads* episode which only required me not to look on the internet in the morning, and stay off the sports channels, but was probably at least as funny as the Ant and Dec remake. It was going swimmingly until half-time in the replay when the directors at Ten Sports obviously thought it was fine to run a sidebar with the latest Champions League tables on. United seemed to have gained an additional point thus confirming that a game that was 2-1 at half-time, finished a draw. Idiots.

Even with a large European contingent in the area there was no evidence of football at all really. Perhaps this was just how it was outside the big cities of the sub-continent that United would initially try to target. However, I'd been told a couple of times before I'd left Britain that India was the next big market for Premier League teams. But if Kerala, a state where football was supposedly the most popular sport, wasn't showing the evidence of this, where was? The back pages of the English language newspapers did carry column inches on Premier League football on an almost daily basis, but the single biggest sports story of all during the week was Diego Maradona's visit to Calcutta, which commanded reams of coverage. Was this evidence of a huge interest in football, or just a response to the first high-profile visitor to the country in the aftermath of the terror strikes? As one fan put it to the BBC, "Calcutta had gone into a shell following the terror alerts. Maradona's visit has erased our fears of a terror strike and Calcutta is back to its noisy self."

Maradona, ever the populist, went ahead with the visit, the huge fee and blanket security he received no doubt helping. While the euphoria of the 20,000 who came out to see him at the Mohun Bagan ground was understandable, the chief of police, Gautam Mohan Chakrabarty's comments that, "Calcuttans are mad about football and they went into a frenzy over Maradona. This was no less than handling a terror strike," were a little irresponsible to say the least.

It was ample evidence of how a fleeting appearance can create a ridiculous hype. Maradona, apparently concerned over the crush he'd faced at the airport, cut his stadium visit down to just seven minutes, failing to stay for a light show about his career, or to deliver on a 45-minute coaching clinic he was due to give. But a few soundbites delivered on the monstrosity of the Mumbai attacks, and his opinions on Barack Obama and George W. Bush, were enough to send the crowd home happy. It was, as a reporter for the *Indian Times* said, all about seeing him live, seeing him in the flesh.

If Indians were all of the same mindset as Benson then Maradona's role as arch-villain (perhaps outside of England he got an easier ride) at the 1990 World Cup would have explained the interest, especially in a football-keen city such as Calcutta. But it mainly highlighted the lure of star power again and that excitement at seeing someone in the flesh. United are yet to make an overtly direct bid for the Indian market by going to play a match there, but Bayern Munich chose the very same stadium to make their debut in the summer of 2008, beating Mohun Bagan 3-0 in front of 120,000 people; an overwhelming turn-out. If United are failing to sell out tour matches in China, then wouldn't India, with a public salivating over the chance to see such stars, not make a far more sensible destination?

Or, are United trying to play it a little cute with this one, as they initially had in China? Instead of steaming in like a Roy Keane challenge, they are avoiding making a rod for their own back, avoiding being expected to turn up every other year to play a game. Instead they are keen as ever here to brand-build. That is why the visits by United are from David Gill, not Wayne Rooney. That's why the recent deal with Airtel to carry United content to mobiles across India and the surrounding region, and deals over DVD distribution have been set up in an attempt to make inroads into the counterfeit goods market. That's why the United bar franchise that had just spread to Bangkok is soon to make its mark in India.

A rising and increasingly affluent middle class is what United and other Premier League clubs are interested in, even if they are trying to dress their interests up in talent searches. Indian national coach Bob Houghton has spoken out over clubs seeing India as a "purely business proposition", and it would be only the most naïve of commentators that saw things otherwise. So while United may team up with Nike to promote an U-14 tournament or conduct a talent search in Goa, and Chelsea might sign an agreement with the AFC, and Liverpool may back a football academy in Pune (these things have all already happened) with the merest hope that they unearth an Indian star, plugging a gaping gap in Premier League football (Bachung Bhutia has come closest, feted in Indian but only ever making it to Bury), it is the clubs themselves and the sale of merchandise that they are promoting. It is not the talent, but the money they are after in an increasingly football-focused country – an emerging market where World Cup rights for South Africa

2010 have been sold for $40m compared to the $2m they fetched back in 2002.

It is that brand-building that seems the new way forward for the club. With no expectation for the team to travel, they are free to promote the brand. It's a change in tactics that's seen them secure big chunks of finance from the likes of Airtel in the Indian sub-continent, Smirnoff in south-east Asia and Saudi Telecom in Saudi Arabia just for the use of game footage and player images on their services and in their promotions. All this designed to push a brand now rated as the eighth most valuable in the sporting world, only behind FIFA and the World Cup in football terms. With this in mind will we ever see United travel to India? I wouldn't have thought it likely anytime soon.

PONDICHERRY
Gamba Osaka (n) 5-3
UK time: 18/12/08, 10.45
Local time: 18/12/08, 16.15

OUR downtime in Kovalam enabled things in the country to settle a little bit and with Rahul, my United contact in Mumbai, keeping us in the loop with the post-terror situation I was really keen to go. Our movement in the south had taken us through Trivandrum, Kanyakumari, Trichy and Pondicherry, before heading to Chennai for our flight to Mumbai.

Post-Kovalam, Pondicherry was the only location we'd be in for a game before we reached Mumbai; United facing Gamba Osaka in the semi-final of the Club World Cup. Known as the French Riviera of the East, the educational hub of Pondicherry houses 24 colleges in its district, perhaps the ideal place for students because of its relatively relaxed drinking laws and easy access to pizzas, burgers and chicken kievs. 'Pondi' as it is affectionately known, also provides a great diversion for tourists, as restaurants cram full of western faces hunting out a taste of home, revelling in the presence of wine that is absent from the rest of India's south.

I lost a little patience with it, though, when the entire town's cable network went down on the day of the match, sending me back to the old text message back-and-forth with my brother to keep me in touch with developments. Clare attempted to console me by claiming that it wasn't a real game. In a way it was true and in the grand scheme of things it was good that I was missing this match rather than any other, but that was little comfort as my phone seemed to be continually buzzing through the 90 minutes. I had, after all, been all but starved of goals lately, missing us hit a total of ten in the last couple of weeks now, only ever seemingly catching 1-0 wins and a goalless draw with Spurs. The final would be an interesting proposition but the 'Champions of the World' sound-bites coming out of the United camp sounded a little bit over the top. Although, I guess if you are trying to make waves in a new market then having FIFA prove that you are the best team on the planet would certainly help turn the heads of the uneducated.

We were due to hit Mumbai a couple of days before the final, but had to get there first. Pondi has no train station, so a short cab-ride to nearby Villupuram was required to make a 5pm departure. There are plenty of horror stories about train delays in India, but having travelled almost exclusively by rail around the south of the country, and yes, many times around the previous countries we had visited, we put this talk down to a bit of traveller exaggeration. Turned out we'd just been lucky.

While the bigger stations in India are upgrading and bringing in the sorts of things we take for granted in the UK, like digital displays and up to the minute train information, plenty of the middle-sized and all the smaller stations still hark back to simpler times. Villupuram was one of the smallest we'd visited. It didn't have any feasible main entrance – we had to cross the tracks to the platform, bypassing a cow – and neglected to even display the handwritten blackboard of departure information we'd witnessed elsewhere.

We managed to establish which platform the train was leaving from, but listening to the announcements over the PA, in three languages, revealed there was to be a delay of an indiscriminate length. A lad, dressed in school uniform, and doing some work in his exercise book told us it wouldn't arrive until 10pm. I thought he'd obviously wrongly overheard our conversation that he wasn't a part of, and naturally hoped that I'd misheard him too. I didn't want to wait outside on a platform for five hours that was for sure.

We sought information from a guard and he told us the train had been delayed, but would be there by 6.15pm. The schoolboy overruled him: "five hours, five hours late. Don't listen to them they don't know anything, I looked before I left home." Surely if he knew it was delayed by five hours and had checked when he was at home he would have just left five hours later? Unless of course he was part of a new-breed of masochistic train watcher interested in finding the day's longest delays and seeking out the psychological damage it wrought on its passengers. Maybe so as he soon jumped on a different train entirely.

Following a number of false alarms, where trains pulled up to the platform only to leave without any change in passengers, we decided to go in search of some other information, successfully finding a small station master's office. "Hi, do you know when the train to Chennai is going to come? It should have been here at 5pm. It's 7.30pm now," I enquired.

The station master, a studious man, dressed resplendently in his white uniform, requested the piece of paper with our reservation information on. He looked at it, he looked at me. He looked at the paper. "Yes," he said slowly, "this train is late."

"Yes, it is."

"The train is late," he repeated handing the paper back to me and returning to his desk.

We waited on the platform. Clare made another attempt to glean some more specific information around 9pm, and got a similar response. I had another go at 10pm. Again the station master requested the piece of paper with our reservation information on. He looked at it, he looked at me. He looked at the paper. "Yes, this train is late." *Oh is it? Why didn't you tell me, I hasn't realised I'd been waiting for five hours, and how do you not recognise me, I'm the only white male in this whole godforsaken station, why do you need the paper again?* I felt like saying.

"Yes, it is. But how late will it be?" I remained polite.

"Maybe an hour. Who knows?"

Who knows? Excellent.

My third try at 11.30pm, also revealed that the "train is late", although there was some slightly more specific news. Apparently it was now due in at 12.15am, but at which platform?

"Who knows?"

Thanks for the help.

It turned up at 12.35am, 7 hours 35 minutes late, before taking an extra two hours longer than scheduled to get to Chennai. Our flight was at midday, so we abandoned our plans to go and pay for a night in a hostel in favour of going straight to the airport. That was the end of our relationship with trains as we vowed to give up our love for rail for the rest of our trip. Cue montage of our best train moments.

MUMBAI
Quito, Club World Cup final (n) 1-0
UK time: 21/12/08, 10.45
Local time: 21/12/08, 16.15

"SO, what about if Sachin Tendulkar moved clubs?" I ventured.

"Sachin Tendulkar would not move clubs."

"Ok, but what if he did?"

"He could not."

"Ok, hypothetically what if Tendulkar moved clubs?"

"Hypothetically, Tendulkar cannot move clubs."

"Alright, someone else." I racked my brains to drag through the minimal cricket knowledge I had. "Ah. What if Dravid moved clubs? Rahul Dravid?"

"Dravid would not move clubs either."

"Ok, but what if he did?"

"He could not."

"Hypothetically?"

"Hypothetically, Rahul Dravid could not move clubs."

This was not merely my attempt to prove that my interviewing skills had failed to move on since Bangkok. The point I was trying to get to as I sat across from Neil Joshi from Mumbai broadsheet *Afternoon* and Rahul Bali from *Goal.com* and more importantly a United fan on his home turf, was the old Asian fascination with star-quality. What I was getting from Neil, though, was a flat refusal to consider comparisons between cricket and football in anyway valid. We'd already discussed that Beckham's move from United had cost them a number of fans in India, but I was trying to go further than that to establish whether this sort of 'club-hopping' would stand up in the face of a move between two big rivals. After the failed cricket analogy, I reversed time and had Beckham, the single best reference point for United throughout the continent, not moving to Real Madrid but to Liverpool. The answer was still the same. Yes, a lot of Indian fans would have followed him. Rahul, though, was keen to state he would not be one of them, believing these people to be fickle, shallow and not real fans, an understatement if ever there was one, and introducing an economy of scale for I could easily say the same about him. Beckham was big news here, though this was undoubtedly a country that took hero worship to another level. I'd seen that to an extent with the Maradona reports, but Rahul's recounting of temples built for cricketers, and of sacrificial fires lit ahead of the cricket World Cup to 'help' the team, proved it went far deeper.

We'd seen it outside the bar we were in, at the top of Colaba Causeway (Mumbai's major commercial vein), a mass of people hording around a cinema, pushing to get in, fighting to be first just to see a film on opening day at one of Mumbai's most popular theatres. It's normal, it seems, for fans to do anything to get close to their 'God' and Rahul was amazingly not at all perturbed by the Calcutta police-chief's comments that controlling the Maradona crowd was similar to post-terror security. Perhaps the need for star-quality was not at its greatest in Japan, maybe it was here in India. It seemed here existed a completely different set of supporter ideals, which made little or no sense to me. But then the whole following United from the other side of the world thing didn't anyway, that was kind of why I was here, what I wanted to get to the bottom of. What was it that brought these people to *my* team?

The analogies with cricket didn't add up at all, and what Benson had told me about the respective popularities of the sports didn't make sense. A small walk around Mumbai, particularly on a Sunday, had revealed road-side games of cricket everywhere – and this was in the most crowded of crowded metropolises. Some were obviously impromptu hits, spontaneous in formation, but others in everything aside from location were more sophisticated, with teams donning kits of their own making, with low-rent name and number printing. It seemed that the presence of a busy main road was not going to get in the way. But a football? Not a sniff of one.

Hockey is actually India's national sport, but cricket had a trigger event that opened the floodgates to mass appeal, that allowed the stars of Tendulkar and Dravid to soar. Winning the 1983 World Cup, followed by clever marketing in the late 80s and early 90s had made cricket what is was. The closest thing that football had in the country, and the reason behind United's popularity was, as Rahul identified, the 1999 Treble. If ever there was a defining event to herald an influx of glory-hunting fans then it was the most successful club season in English football history. Thus the Indian love affair with United went against everything that 'loyal' football fans are supposed to be. It was a deadly mix of fickleness and trophy hugging – a long-term recipe for disaster. Or so we Brits believe.

However, there were similarities between myself and Rahul, and credit him for his dedication now, no matter how he got to supporting the team in the first place. He was, as many a fan knows, in the awkward position of putting off social events, meetings and clearing calendars to make way for football. Anyone new to being a football fan or to their dedicated ways will, of course, find this strange at first, but people soon learn there's no point inviting you to weddings, parties or other social events if it coincides with a game, you will quite simply take no prisoners. Rahul was dedicated in that respect, with the games at stranger times for him too (but the most convenient of the major European leagues), he was confident in saying he watched all of them. There were surprising points of familiarity as well; he was versed on needing to avoid the term 'Man U' for instance, and, like me, disliked watching games in pubs in the main because it prevents you from really appreciating what's going on in the match (I never find this at live games); although it obviously affected him more than me as he was busy talking as Rooney scored the winner against Quito.

We chatted through the course of the game, covering a range of United-related topics; the relevance of the Club World Cup for instance (he, too, saw it as of little real importance), the 39th game proposition (he pleasingly realised it was stupid, but said so because the games are for the English audience, which appears utterly contradictory). He was naturally keen to fight his corner and defend other Indian United fans. He obviously knew his very modern history, and made interesting points, but there was evidently a disconnection in the ideals of fandom. He had little knowledge of the club's ownership or the realisation of the importance of ticket pricing, freely admitting that he simply didn't know – although he said there had been protests about the takeover in Mumbai.

This was all interesting stuff, yet it was stuff that I'd expected to find. I wasn't really here to find this out. I was here to find out why. Well, 'why' was because of the connection with the team, borne out of success. I knew that, so perhaps it wasn't so much 'why', it was more: 'what's the point'?

What is the point? I could muse on the nature of fandom, I could theorise about the psychology of the football fan, but it's not really new. I think to me, I guess it's not merely an interest, that's why you get so pissed off, that's why the highs last so long, it's actually a part of your make-up. That's why it has to be organic, I don't think you can just inject yourself with a new chunk of character. You can develop an interest, sure, but to me and many other football fans you merely develop an interest in something like trains or fishing, not an overriding support of a football team. That's why I struggled to understand the point for these new Reds. It's not entertainment at the level of *your* team, it's raw emotion. A Real Madrid v Barca game gets me excited for the entertainment, the quality of the football, I'll go out of my way to watch it. Seeing *your* team is different. It's not a jolly day-out, it isn't entertaining as such. You go to be a part of one living, breathing organism. It's a special, individual relationship, yet you're not an individual you're a part of a collective – that's what makes it so important – important that if you are a fan, you are interested in the issues that fans are interested in – like ticketing and ownership and the direction of the club. You cannot exclude those from the on-pitch events.

You can understand why someone like Rahul would end up with United. The club fill a void, make up for something that India cannot provide – a stadium, an atmosphere. He said that's what attracts people to the Premier League. This is what United are exploiting in Asia; this is why they have a chance of sorts; that's why they don't go headlong into Germany, Italy or even Russia. If you want to be interested in football then it is natural that you'd find your way to a highly publicised and broadcasted league, but to say that ownership and ticketing are not important to you, belies naïvety. These are the issues that could dictate whether the club survives, whether the very full stadiums that lead to the attraction remain full. In light of this, describing the attitude that I possibly have to United fans as an 'English snobbishness' was interesting, while Rahul's statement that fans in Korea, India and Iraq are now as important to the club as anyone in Manchester, because it's now a world game, is simply not true. Unfortunately at times the club views it like this, but if a season ticket holder pays close to £1,000 to attend league and cup games in a season, then as an individual he is more important to the club's longevity than 1,000 fans abroad that the club tried to flog 50 Ronaldo jerseys to before he hightailed it to Spain.

It's hard to capture that essence of being a 'fan', of what it means, what it should mean. But thinking about what Rahul was saying was perhaps leading me to examine my own relationship with the club, what it meant to me, more than what it meant to him. Contradictions are rife in these discussions merely because the ideals are so intangible and probably because people don't actually spend that much time examining it. The point for me, when it comes down to it, is the going to the game, so did that mean I needed something back to maintain my interest? No, but the match itself was a reward of sorts, Rahul, watching from afar, was getting nothing in that sense, aside from 'the satisfaction of watching your team do well.' Was this just over-analysing? Was he right, is it a global game? No. I just wasn't convinced. But what did I want him to say? 'Yes Tim, that's true, I waste all my time on nothingness. You are a real fan. In fact I shouldn't support them at all.' Well, kind of, yeah.

But maybe that was part of a superiority complex that I had about it, it had, after all, been clear here, and would again be at points later, that the people I'd met were trying to 'impress' me with their depth of knowledge or their level of support as though I could validate it in some way with my match-going credentials and geographical family history that they couldn't replicate. But to me supporting your club is not about proving something to someone else. To me it's about an inherent value that sees you back your team to the hilt and, yes, attend matches – which is obviously impossible for many of the millions of United fans who live abroad (although many do make the pilgrimage when they can).

Again the differences were down to culture perhaps, and that's why a discussion like this will never really end, or come to a point of conclusion. Was I just viewing it all too negatively anyway, taking it all too seriously? After all had it not been for United then Rahul and I would never have met, we wouldn't have been together in the bar in Mumbai, watching the Club World Cup final together, I wouldn't have learnt about this perspective, and without wanting to go all dewy-eyed over it, is football not supposed to be a unifying force rather than a disparate one?

We would probably never reach a point of agreement (and, in fact, it's a debate we still continue by email today), so it was very easy for me to say, with history and authenticity on my side, that I was right, and Rahul was wrong. But that shouldn't affect my opinions of him as a person. It is necessary to disassociate the fan from the man. Perhaps football, like politics and religion, is the third spoke to the wheel of conversation you should avoid, but that would lose the enjoyment of a discussion like this. That is what football is all about isn't it?

This whole thing was confusing me, it wasn't making things clearer. Bloody trips to expand your horizons and free your opinions simply muddied the waters further – that was the only solid opinion I had come to thus far, that was for sure.

UNIVERSITY had allowed Rahul to explore his football/United interest with others as this is where the game is most popular in India; football is viewed as fashionable and a good degree of the preoccupation is down to the players' images and their lifestyles. It was our shared interest that had allowed me to meet up with Rahul in his home city, at a time of recent crisis for Mumbai, and spend an enjoyable afternoon with him and Neil. They thanked us for still visiting the city despite the recent terrorist events. The irony of me being in his country as a tourist, and in effect accusing him of being a 'football tourist' was not wholly lost on either of us. I guess it all comes down to perspective; what yours is and retaining a sense of one.

Rahul, Clare and I all left shortly after United had declared themselves the World Champions. We strolled up Colaba – the best place to get a glimpse of the city at its dirty, claustrophobic, people-throbbing best. This was what I'd imagined Indian cities to really be like. It bubbled with life, even on a Sunday when many places remained shut. It was Rahul's first visit to the area since 26 November, when he'd very nearly got caught up in the shootings that took place at Leopold's Café. He'd been walking up Colaba with some footballers from a local side, a few of whom had gone to an Adidas show room nearby. Rahul and Jaspal Singh, one of the players, had strolled past the café, and Rahul had considered going in for a drink, only continuing because Singh didn't want to stop. They made it only 20 yards before the shooting started. As Rahul put it, after realising they weren't firecrackers, they "ran for [their] lives". They made it to the Adidas showroom where the other players were and Rahul dragged the metal shutters down for protection.

Despite the close proximity of events and the effect it must have had on him, he had no real problems relaying the story, pointing out where the gunmen had stood as we walked up the causeway. Had he been nervous, he didn't really show it, and was admirably philosophical about things, and was, rightly, impressed with his own actions that night; how he managed to help people get away from the scene. Having this discussion immediately after the football debate again left me with pause for thought. Is football really that important? Even now it was just a few weeks on from the attacks, but there was little sign of the events of that Sunday on Colaba, where fake United shirts hung in stalls. It seemed strange that people didn't keep stopping and just thinking about what had happened. Mumbai's ability to heal and move on was, Rahul believed, one of its best and worst faculties, but that power for regeneration also remains a hallmark of Manchester United. Was Rahul's connection with the club deeper than he thought, or is that too much of a stretch?

Rahul admits now that it was strange to return to the scene where he'd heard bullets, and seen blood on the road, and to re-tell the events. Colaba had moved on, but preoccupation with the events elsewhere in the city remained as people visited the Taj Mahal Palace hotel, still closed when we were there, just to get a glimpse of where the drama had unfolded. The juxtaposition of what was important to me, and what was important to Rahul, and how in many respects they were the same was revealing. He declined to eat with us after the walk up Colaba, I think perhaps because we were heading back down the same road. After we had parted Clare mentioned we may have given him the impression we were going to go to Leopold's, so who can blame him.

Rahul's presence certainly heightened our reactions to events and again this terrorism felt more dangerous than that in England. It was strange. Was it because of where we were, or because we knew someone who'd been caught up in it? Did the proximity of the events make me feel football was any less important to me? It probably should have done – but it didn't – I wasn't thinking about it in those terms. United had actually enabled me to meet Rahul in the first place and learn more about the situation than I ever would from British media that had initially inferred the attacks had al-Qaeda origins. Speculation in India now suggested the link between targets had been TATA – ironically a mega-conglomerate that had been linked with United as a replacement for shirt sponsor, AIG. I was determined that United should be a unifying force in my mind from now on, there were enough divisions in the world, creating more over a common interest was ridiculous, surely. Shit, I wasn't finding myself was I?

DELHI
Stoke (a) 1-0
UK time: 26/12/08, 12:45
Local time: 26/12/08, 18:15

Middlesbrough (h) 1-0
UK time: 29/12/08, 20:00
Local time: 30/12/08, 01:30

DELHI'S Connaught Place is made up of three concentric circles, each representing a 'ring'. All contain buildings, mainly businesses, separated by ring roads, and the whole thing is divided into eight sections desig-nated by the radial roads that spread out from the centre. Amongst these many businesses are a few big hotels that would surely offer Christmas dinners of some sort. As much as you travel to try and explore foreign culture, Clare and I had decided that a couple of days revelling in the comforts of home would be a superb way to recharge the adventurous mindset, before heading off to Rajasthan and Agra.

The hotels on Connaught Place were a lot more expensive than our overpriced guesthouse set on one of the outer rings, and looked far too pricey for a dinner. Phoning around brought no real luck because we'd managed to lounge around until about 2pm on the day, watching Christmas films and many of the hotels that were serving Christmas buffets were finishing up at 3pm. Our only remaining option, the only place that was attempting to recreate a Christmas experience, was TGI Fridays. When you can order a set menu that comes with a free glass of wine, you know you're onto a winner. Of all the food that we ate on the entire trip, I class this as comfortably the worst thing I put in my mouth – and we ate fermented Yak's milk in Mongolia. In fact the only remotely edible things were the mushrooms. What? You didn't have mushrooms with your Christmas dinner?! Bet you didn't have potato skins to start with either. The authentic Christmas experience indeed.

Would Boxing Day football get any closer to the real thing? We'd done our Christmas television watching on the day itself and were going to give the second Christmas dinner that you might enjoy on the 26th a bit of a miss – although I'd have killed for a real turkey sandwich. We decided to go back on the sightseeing trail, racking up the Indira Gandhi museum, the Gandhi memorial, the Humalayan Tomb and Pira Qila fort, all before the early kick-off back home against Stoke. Internet research had revealed a couple of sports bars in the capital, one of which, the All Sports Bar, was just down the road from us on Connaught Place and which according to a news-piece dating from just 26 May 2008, was the first sports bar in the capital and boasted 22 huge plasma screens. In Beijing the bars I'd found had been slightly off the beaten track, in south-east Asia they'd been a by-product of tourism, even in Tokyo the bar had been tucked away in a corner, and was more of a fashionable hangout than your average sports bar, but here in New Delhi, it was slap-bang in the middle of the bustling business centre, making it the first bar that'd I'd found actually directed at natives rather than tourist communities, or ex-pat, niche markets.

All Sports' plans were certainly ambitious, and entailed opening 500 branches across the country over the course of five years (there remain only two, 12 months on from their second opening – what did Stalin teach us about 5-year plans people?). Its marketing slant was interesting too. There were familiar lines about solving fights over the remote and, in a very Indian way, there were opportunities to 'keep spirits high' sidestepping any sensitivity over drinking. It did attempt to mark out its 'in-stadia' feel too, a very salient point, given the evident problem with going to a match. It all seemed an attempt to tap into the western culture of watching sport in large groups and drinking.

Inside, it turned out that we'd instantly located the whereabouts of all of India's Christmas decorations, and clearly we should have joined them the previous day. It looked an impressive place, and if you were looking for a bar to watch sport in this was it. Big screens plastered the walls and each booth had its own set on which you could select whatever channel you desired. They even had their own All Sports newspaper, with the latest Premier League news; a lovely concept, except it was about two months out of date.

They were less tactful about their liking for drink once in the safety of the bar too. Each table had place mats listing the range of drinks offers across the week; enough to cause anti-binge drinking campaigners in the UK to reach for the bottle. Amongst the highlights were 'bottomless beer' where you were invited to 'try your limits, by drinking as much as you can' in a limited space of time, and free drinks for all ladies on a Wednesday night. Ah, the sign of an upmarket joint if ever there was one. We were drinking during the rather boring 2 for 1 promotion on bottles of Fosters, but still we had a booth with our own television.

We needn't have bothered getting there too early, though, as the custom was a little bit thin on the ground, but we didn't manage to position ourselves far enough away from another English couple. The pair painfully blundered their way through the entire match, speaking at a ludicrously high volume. She ran through the gamut of clichéd United chats; who would be the next manager (she had a feeling that it'd be Cantona – it won't); doesn't Wayne Rooney look like Shrek? (no). He told her about the Ji-Sung Park chant (she didn't know), then he asked her whether he'd be able to get tickets for his Dad, who was a lifelong fan who'd never been to a game (always a good indicator), but she thought it'd be absolutely impossible (wrong again). The game itself mattered little to them, although they did offer the odd pearl of wisdom (for instance Rooney crossing slightly beyond Tevez was apparently an "open chance"), but then when United finally broke down Stoke's resilience they celebrated more than anyone. Was it just because they were English that they had to falsify this devotion to the game?

Personally I was delighted with the goal, it had been a bit of a war of attrition, and my brother and I simultaneously texting each other 'thank Christ for that' displayed the measure of relief. Meanwhile, Clare had managed to spend most of the game on the phone to various friends and relatives passing on Christmas wishes. She really wasn't getting the point of coming to watch these matches.

The final match during our first stay in Delhi was a win over Middlesbrough, watched through one eye in our room, finishing as it did at 3.15am. We were leaving for Agra and the Taj Mahal at 6.30 in the morning and I really did think about just not watching that game. In the end I couldn't bring myself to do it, and battled on regardless.

RAJASTHAN
Southampton (a) 3-0
UK time: 04/01/09, 16:00
Local time: 04/01/09, 21:30

Derby (a) 0-1
UK time: 07/01/09, 19:45
Local time: 08/01/09, 01:15

THE Chelsea game on 11 January was looming on the horizon, and there was quite simply no way I was going to put myself in a position where I could possibly miss it. After juggling smaller matches, it was time for me to make demands. We were heading off on a trip around Rajasthan, India's biggest state, visiting the likes of Jaisalmer, Jaipur, Udaipur (all famous for their forts), as well as a side-trip to Agra for the pearl in the crown, the Taj Mahal. As we were then due to fly out of Delhi to Kenya on the 14th, to go on safari, I wanted to make sure we were back in the capital by the 11th so that I could watch the Chelsea match minus any pre-match stress caused by a hunt for a television. With this small window, travelling by train on a daily basis seemed an absolute nightmare, and anyway we'd banished rail travel following our delay in Villupuram. So in the end we hired a car and a driver for the 13-day trip for a ridiculously low rate of £25 a day. It was a whistle-stop tour through another very different India. This was a world away from the hard-drinking All Sports Bar of Delhi and the multi-cultural grittiness of Mumbai. The best English equivalent would be a farming community, but that comparison does little to capture the remote nature of the place. Imagine, for instance, cows wandering everywhere; in the middle of the roads blocking cars, walking around the streets, butting English tourists trying to buy some shampoo from a chemist, revelling in their sacred status.

It was, as our driver kept summarising, "traditional". He, for instance, came from somewhere close to Jodphur, a place where his wife would not work, and his ambitions for his children eventually to go to university would be frowned upon. Living in Delhi for work was his only chance to eat meat, something he admitted to hiding from his mother. It was a sensitive part of the country, bordering Pakistan, particularly Jalsaimer where we stayed just 20km from the border, and fighter jets flew over on an hourly basis. We were not to worry though, they were "just planning the war" – all part of the political blame game which followed the Mumbai attacks.

Obviously there were degrees of difference throughout the region. From Udaipur with its palace popular with James Bond fanatics for its role in *Octopussy* to Puskhar where all meat, alcohol and dairy products are banned, to the stately Taj Mahal which with a construction time of 12 years, narrowly beats Wembley as the most exhaustive early episode of *Grand Designs*. It was wholly different to the rest of the country, clinging to authenticity, the last bastion of Indian tradition if you will, and thus the last place to invite the overtures of Manchester United. It seemed unlikely that anyone visiting or living there would have had their mind on the events that I did. The saving grace in India, though, is that every single hostel, even when you're paying just £6 a night for a double room, comes with a TV, with an array of channels. We were even living it up, paying around a tenner for our room in Udaipur, so it wasn't the lack of television that was the problem, the United v Southampton game just wasn't being shown (I later found that it was carried by a subscription movie channel – Sony Pix). However, I did manage to stay up for the first leg of the League Cup semi-final against Derby and 'enjoyed' another night of three hours sleep. This was now getting tough in the sleep stakes, which impacted on my desire to keep to my stated aim of not missing a game if I could help it.

DELHI – part II
Chelsea (h) 3-0
UK time: 11/01/09, 16.00
Local time: 11/01/09, 21.30

FROM the Manutd.com messageboard.

'I am writting as a man utd fan who lives in melbourne.a person who if he ever went within europe would certantly want to see man untd play football at home. cuz the last time I went it was too long ago . Anyway . . . I think of hostile really reluctant home crowds like those of fenebarche sukru sarocglu, Barcelona nou camp,and those Scousers!!!!!!!!!! and Old trafford.

It has been called the theatre of dreams, an inspirational fortress. The only time when i could really hear the crowd through the TV was when we played Barca On That amazing nght. other than that nothing which makes my blood rise or the commentator refer to it. im not for a second saying its not loud.i know how loud it can get.

But for chelsea on Sunday PLZ cheer for me , every Manutd fan around the world and most importantly our players.it would be amazing if it reached the atmposphere against The catalans.If it does i would bet my life that we would win. the 12th man . . . maybe its cuz weve been a bit shaky so fans around the world are to nervouss to really Cheer!!!!!!!. but if i was any were in england ,or somehow at the ground Id make sure my lungs would pop,and they would have to call the parametics. i would rather loose my voice for the whole year .then see us loose against Chelski lol.'

It's remarkable how a 'supposed' shared interest in the club can bring you closer to a person, help you get somewhere and experience new things, as I've said already – but yet at the same time it can also make you realise how far detached you can be from these idiots. It goes without saying that having been sent this missive shortly before the Chelsea game, I was in no mood to attempt to chat to any 'fans' that I happened to bump into. This was to be all about the football, about me watching it, and nothing else really. Football, or rather your club, can make you very single-minded. The bigger the game, the less distraction you want, the more you want to focus on events. Those who don't understand might say, 'you're not playing in the match, what are you talking about?' But if you don't get it then . . . you just don't get it. That's your problem more than mine.

This was a big game for United, a game we really needed to win. It could be enjoyable, it could be hellish. It was the biggest game that I'd missed since leaving. With away tickets invariably 'chubbed', your only guarantee is attendance at home games. I'd begun to make my peace with the games that I was missing, accepting it, only really thinking of where we'd be and how I could watch them now. There wasn't a weekly dissection of my not attending anymore. This was completely different. I was pissed off to be honest; the anxiety, the impending excitement was all replaced with a foul mood – as I'm sure Clare will testify. This was hurting. I'd sold my ticket for the portion of the season that I was missing to my brother's fiancée; she was complicit in this, being a South African and all. She didn't really deserve to be at the game. Did it matter this was my fault? My doing? I wasn't even considering it now to be honest. This was a big game in league terms, but it was Chelsea; imagine how I was going to feel come Liverpool's visit in March. Football is a wholly selfish activity from a spectating point of view, it's all about saying, 'I was there'. That's why, for instance, the entire population of Scotland claims to have been at the 7-3 European Cup final between Real Madrid and Eintracht Frankfurt in 1960. Saying, 'I could have been there, but I was in India' is not quite the same.

If you can't get a ticket that's one thing, there's an external factor stopping you from going, but when you have a ticket as I did, but have given it up, that's different entirely. You feel guilty, you feel disloyal and you feel scared of missing something. I would be missing out tonight, I knew that. I didn't want to miss out at all. I actually didn't want it to be a good game. I wanted it to be scrappy, boring, awful – belying a lack of loyalty to people at the stadium, to my friends and family. I didn't want United to lose by any means. No. Definitely not. But I wanted it to be 1-0, a scrappy set-piece or something. What if it was 5-0, the culmination of all of Ferguson's work over 20 years in one game, and I missed it, because of something crap like 7 months of travelling? Unthinkable. So, rather than tell Clare I held her responsible for me not being at the game, I hid all this in a strop.

In the circumstances there was no way that I was going to try and dissect the mindset of those turning up to watch the game. There wouldn't be many anyway, there hadn't been last time we'd watched a game at the All Sports Bar, and as Rahul had said, "they aren't interested in football in Delhi." But, ten minutes before kick-off, the place was packed, upstairs and downstairs, and almost all of those present, except for Clare and I, were wearing some form of United encrested clothing.

As was noticeable at the 2002 World Cup, where it was common to hear screams as soon as the ball neared the goal, there were noticeable differences in 'viewing' culture here. People were enjoying themselves, sure, but it felt like an audience not fully understanding the ebb and flow of the game, fearing danger to the United goal when there was none, and expecting people to score from ridiculous places and showing discontent when they failed to do so. When United seemingly opened the scoring through Cristiano Ronaldo, the place went a bit mental. It seemed I was the only one who noticed that it had been disallowed. When we scored immediately anyway, I joined in the general exuberance as music blared from the speakers. The one-sided nature of the support; the 'innocence' of the crowd; the music; it all felt a little like *Gladiators* rather than a clash between two Premier League title contenders.

United were playing pretty damn well. As the game progressed the exuberance increased, and I found strangely that I was thoroughly enjoying it. Of course, I should have been enjoying it, United were hammering Chelsea, but I was actually enjoying watching it here. In this place. This clouded the issue – I wanted more goals, I was getting pleasure from being a part of these hammed up celebrations (no doubt in part this was because this was the best game I'd watched since I'd been away). Football should bring joy, collective joy and it should be fun – it is sport after all. These spectators were enjoying it for what it was. I was swept up in the euphoria for the entire duration of the 90 minutes. There was no prominently obnoxious attitude, there was none of the whingeing at players, the questioning of their motives that you get in England. People came along simply to enjoy it and they did. For the cynical amongst us this ultimately tells of potential unquestioned loyalty, and indeed the lack of cynicism amongst these supporters makes them ripe for the Glazer PR machine, but for one match I sat back, or jumped up and down, and just enjoyed it.

The win also meant that I was no longer in a bad mood, I was elated. I was happy, I was drunk. It was the best we'd played all season, and . . . and . . . I'd missed it. There was still that nudge of regret, that little thing that stopped me from fully revelling in the occasion. I felt a distinct lack of animosity to the people I'd shared the bar with; they had on this occasion only gone to enhance my enjoyment of events. It wasn't the in-stadia feel the All Sports Bar had hoped for, but it was a remarkable scene. The bar was basically a slice of the west in the middle of Delhi. Football in India it seemed was actually indicative of the fight between the culture and tradition of a Rajasthan and the new generation who patronise the All Sports Bar who want to break out and escape the claustrophobia, the 'tradition'. Manchester United represent the most tangible and accesible part of the west that they can grab on to, bringing with it the liberating feeling of being part of something, a movement, and perhaps easy access to a drinking culture, something which is very new in India. For these people, being a United fan becomes a point of identity, a badge of the future. I began to wonder if this was a sign of the Indian weekends to come.

That was that where football and India were at for us. After celebrating helping load the gun later used to fire Big Phil, we were leaving for another country, another continent. The next match, a home game against Wigan, would be on the 14th, and we'd be in Kenya, awaiting the start of our safari. That's what we thought anyway – a text message was about to change all of that.

East Africa

SOMEWHERE IN AFRICA
Wigan (h) 1-0
UK time: 14/01/09, 20.00
Local time: 14/01/09, 23.00

'SOMEWHERE IN AFRICA' might seem like the lazy stereotyping of an American television drama, so perhaps 'should have been Nairobi' would be a more accurate assessment of my attempts to watch the United v Wigan match in Kenya's capital, being swept away by an introduction to 'African time'. It wasn't all Africa's fault, given that the delays started in India, but it seemed to be the catchphrase on everybody's lips when we finally landed in the world's second largest continent.

I'd found that not having the name of a pub or bar to watch a game in was at least misguided, so not knowing what continent we were going to be in was downright careless. It wasn't our fault admittedly but it emphasised that we weren't exactly living the nomadic lifestyle. Instead we remained tethered to home by the familiar and all-pervading structure of the fixture list, the one thing that was always unmovable and that above all others could be jeopardised by such a delay.

Our flight from Delhi to Nairobi, via Addis Ababa, had been scheduled to leave at 1.30am on the morning of the Wigan game. Indian airport security had been cranked up to the max following the terror attacks, meaning international flights now required a lengthy four-hour check-in time, and having checked-out of our hotel at noon we had a long wait ahead. Seven-and-a-half hours into that wait I checked my phone and found four text messages, all from the same unrecognised number, indicating our first flight had been knocked-back by five hours and consequently our connection had been moved to the following day.

A phone call to the airline confirmed the scenario, but as we'd been hanging around for nearly nine hours already, done all we wanted to in Delhi and just finished dinner we decided we may as well go to the airport. Despite the apparent rescheduling, the flight was still listed on screens at the original time and no member of staff seemed to know any differently and we were ushered inside, bypassing new security protocols dictating passengers were held outside the terminal until four hours before take-off. We squeezed through the barricades passing the huge crowds that were gathered outside the building, highlighting for a final time in our stay the mistaken English belief that we're the world leaders in queuing. If there's so much as a hint of an opportunity to queue, Indians will take it up. If that queue ever moves so there's a chance to push, run or in general hurry for something, time-dependent or not, they will surge forward quicker than Alan Shearer at a pile of cash. That's why instead of relaxing in the café, or just standing on the other side of the road, hordes of people, who it wouldn't have surprised me to find didn't even have a flight to catch, jammed up against the crash barriers that marked the perimeter of the terminal building.

Predictably check-in didn't open and at midnight on the dot there was an announcement that the flight would be delayed until 6.20am – they'd sent us that information about five hours ago by text, why only update the staff now? We'd been at the airport since half nine, we were now going to be there another six hours, not to mention the wait on the other end in Addis Ababa. Watching the match at all was in the balance – it was one game I couldn't plan for.

I was already texting home to make sure I'd be getting news as goals went in as soon as I got off a plane somewhere along the line. Text messages about football were my major communications home during our trip – United providing my strongest link, even with my family. The topics were not where I'd been or what I'd seen, they were 'great goal', 'well, that was a bit close for comfort' and 'is Berbatov purposely trying to stop people liking him?'

At 2.30am they opened check-in and we learnt that the airline would be putting us up at a hotel in Addis Ababa, but that the flight was being knocked back another three hours, making it a full 12-hour delay. You kind of expect this on a trip at some point, and sod's law it would happen when a game was on. As we finally trudged to the plane at about 8.30am a woman at the gate pointed to us a few places down the line, saying "there they are" before coming over to drag us to the front. We appeared to be getting upgraded purely on account of being the only white people boarding. Although it was only half eight, and we'd missed a night's sleep, it seemed ungrateful not to accept the offer of champagne as we took our seats, although noticeably the real business-class passengers all opted for orange juice.

A much more comfortable seat afforded us a better chance to grab some sleep, but it did little to dent the tiredness. We waited for two hours in Addis Ababa for a free visa, unable to reclaim our bags because they were in transit, before getting on the bus to take us to the hotel. We both occupied a hypnotic, robotic state by this point, just going where we were told, eager for some sleep and a shower. The hotel room pleasingly had a Supersport channel which I hoped would show the game. I didn't have the strength or the desire to start looking for any other locations; we had to be up again at 6am. Whether I'd manage to stay awake was another matter.

As kick-off approached there was no sign of football. I should've just turned it off and gone to sleep but it felt as though I had a point to prove now. I was going to watch it. If it didn't come on then at least I'd tried my hardest. Miraculously a minute before kick-off, as I readied the remote on the cusp of the blissful sleep I needed, the picture changed – clearly operated by a set of central controls elsewhere in the hotel. The United game was on, hmm, Wigan . . . great. Soon after it started I fell asleep. I awoke spasmodically throughout the match watching five minutes here, five minutes there. I can't recall anything about it at all. I know I saw the goal because it was in the first minute, but that's about it. But I do recall asking myself during one brief waking moment, *why am I doing this exactly?*

SOMEWHERE IN AFRICA ON SAFARI

Bolton (a) 1-0
UK time: 17/01/09, 15.00
Local time: 17/01/09, 18.00 (Lake Navasha, Kenya)

Derby (h) 4-2
UK time: 20/01/09, 20.00
Local time: 20/01/09, 23.00 *(Lake Navasha, Kenya)*

Tottenham (h) 2-1
UK time: 24/01/09, 17.15
Local time: 24/01/09, 20.15 *(Somewhere in Tanzania)*

West Brom (a) 5-0
UK time: 27/01/09, 19.45
Local time: 27/01/09, 22.45 *(Dar es Salaam)*

Everton (h) 1-0
UK time: 31/01/09, 17.30
Local time: 31/01/09, 20.30 *(Zanzibar)*

SOMETIMES YOU HAVE to resign yourself to the inevitable and I did that by agreeing to go on safari. I'd had my way with the Chelsea game, making sure we were in Delhi for it, but safari was the single thing that Clare wanted to do above all else on the trip, so I knew it was coming. It would last for two weeks. Two weeks of camping in remote parts of east Africa as we travelled through Kenya and Tanzania, two weeks of living 'rough' without connection to modern amenities, two weeks without United. As 14-day spans of the football season go, it wasn't a bad one to pick; two Premier League games against unglamorous opposition, a League Cup semi-final and a fourth round FA Cup tie – it was unlikely to shape our season. Yes, a semi-final was amongst them, but it seemed inevitable that against Championship Derby, United would overturn the 1-0 deficit at Old Trafford with ease.

Sweeping through two countries in just a fortnight in an open-sided safari truck proved a great way of viewing the landscape and absorbing the atmosphere of the smaller villages and towns that connected the major landmarks or attractions. What was instantly noticeable throughout and even on our first day's drive from Nairobi to Lake Navasha was the presence of the Premier League. I was honestly taken aback by its prominence in this supposed wilderness.

Asia is the target, we are told. Football's popularity there dictates that. But compared to east Africa, or Kenya and Tanzania at least, it doesn't come close. Asia boasts one third of the entire population of the earth and is slowly but surely getting the money to match, telling its own tale of the reason why clubs are trying to crack the region. Shock, horror. The countless stories telling you that to make an instant friend in Japan or Korea all you need do is start a conversation about Manchester United obviously do start to eat away at you a little bit, and you do begin to think Asia is football's new home. But in Africa the game is everywhere. Every tenth person seems to be in a kit, and not just one club's – there's United, Chelsea, Arsenal, Barcelona, Madrid, AC Milan – although Premier League tops dominate. There are Premier League badges painted on vehicles, entire buses decked out in club colours, and signs everywhere outside small, brightly-painted stone buildings – that pass for watering holes here – advertising the next match. I hadn't expected this at all.

The other 'surprise' was that United weren't the major side here. There were plenty of United jerseys and a 'United bus' somewhere along the line, but it was Arsenal that were most popular. If counting the sheer number of shirts is an accurate indicator, which presumably it is in a culture where wearing your club colours is so important, then Arsenal were definitely the biggest team around here. That realisation produced a strange feeling. I wasn't expecting to find United weren't the number one club and indeed if it had been Real Madrid or Juventus that they'd been losing out to then fine – but to not be the biggest Premier League club, I was actually quite disappointed. I realised this didn't make much sense. Maybe I did take some pride from this 'biggest club in the world' PR after all.

In reality it was good to see this variety of shirts though, for the clubs at least. The very problem with United in China was trying to promote themselves as the be-all and end-all of football. Here in east Africa it was like the Premier League had been exported *en masse*. There were real rivalries and with that came debate, banter and loyalty; hallmarks of what we would call European football culture. It may not have extended much beyond the big sides and the likes of Newcastle, who'd obviously had 'success' in the Premier League years, but it was still better than any club being a lone ranger out here. After all where better for tribe-like football support to organically develop and thrive than Africa?

The flip side of our fast movement was that our destinations were taken out of our hands, and living in a bubble with ten other English tourists meant that it was hard to get a genuine feel for the idiosyncrasies of each place outside of game reserves, campsites and fleeting visits to towns ultimately leading to a few footballing generalisations. It was the case that, aside from the closest safari park and what wildlife it contained, we lost a sense of geographical perspective, highlighting one of the major disadvantages of a group trip like this. It was a strange feeling after our previous four months but we weren't about to stroll into the middle of the Masai Mara on our own and try and track a lion.

The group dynamic on such a trip is, of course, relatively important, as ultimately it can determine your enjoyment and thus first impressions are pretty important. Much to Clare's dismay, I was willing to jeopardise quite a lot of that on the first day when I found that our campsite at Lake Navasha wasn't quite as barebones as I'd thought it would be. They had a swimming pool, they had shower blocks, and yes, they had a bar.

"Maybe we should go for a drink?" I announced shortly before dinner to a few of the strange faces we sat around trying to get to know. There were a few nods of agreement; none of them aware of my real motives.

"You only want to go and see if they can show the football," Clare harrumphed, but despite her meddling the project gained a few allies and so off we went. While there was none of the 22 huge plasma screens of Delhi, the bar did have one television and plenty of sports channels. We persuaded the barman to switch over from the Chelsea game and with a bottle of Tusker, Kenya's beer of choice, in hand we settled in. I chatted to the guy behind the bar who told me he was an Arsenal fan primarily because he liked their style of play. I told him my joke about Kenya having the 'Big 5' (lion, elephant, rhino, leopard and buffalo) while England had their 'Big 4'. It surprisingly went down a storm.

We were called for dinner five minutes before the end of the first half, excellent timing, and the six of us returned to the camp where we sat around a fire to eat. It was the end of our first day on safari. We'd already been out on the lake and seen the hippos that lived nearby. People were clearly excited about what lay ahead and keen to get to know the others in the group. I wolfed my food down, while others took their time, making chit-chat between mouthfuls. It was a delicate situation, I was fidgety, but Clare kept looking at me and shaking her head; this wasn't the time to throw in another casual drink idea. People may have taken the original one with a pinch of salt but realising they didn't know me at all I doubted they'd perfect the same nonchalance to me leaving while they were all eating.

I knew my next move could shape the next two weeks with these people, but equally this indecision was costing me match time. Linda, a mother of children of a similar age to me, leaned over and said, "If you want to go Tim, you should just go." Ah . . . I obviously hadn't hidden it that well then. Needing no further heeding, I bounded from my seat, but without any of my previous allies.

Well, all accept for the barman. I got back to the bar with 65 minutes on the clock, and he seemed to be waiting for my return. "Your team is not doing so well," he happily announced when I walked in.

"Don't worry, we'll be fine," I assured him, and we were, just. Despite his liking for Arsenal, the barman was at my side slapping me on the back moments after I'd been imploring Tevez to "give it" just as he crossed for Berbatov to grab a 90th minute winner.

"You were saying 'give it, give it'. And he gave it," he chuckled, deriving enjoyment from my noticeable pleasure; this was a strange rivalry. The barman clearly loved his football and assured me that in the pubs in the cities around Kenya there would be 'riots' during each match as everyone had their own team. Football is by no means the niche sport that it really remains in Asia, where people like Rahul had to be in a university environment, or similar, with the variety of people and interests that brings, to find someone to speak to about it. Here football is, as in England, an all-consuming passion. Emias, our safari leader, for instance, was from Zimbabwe, and yes he was working for an English company, and yes of course part of his job was to be friendly to those on his safari, but he immediately enquired what the score had been when I returned to the truck. I told him, 1-0. "Ah . . . that means they are top now doesn't it?" It did indeed. When I asked him which team he supported, he didn't have one, and wasn't in his own words a "big football fan". Yet he knew exactly what was going on at the top of the English Premier League.

Pete, another of the crew, spent much of one journey looking over my shoulder as I read through a copy of *World Soccer*; in the end I gave up and just handed him the magazine. I didn't see it again for two days, and that included him fobbing me off when I tried to get it back. He was a fan of Samuel Eto'o and thus, at that point at least, followed Barcelona (although presumably he has moved on, with his hero, to Inter Milan), while Batchi, our cook, liked Chelsea because of Didier Drogba. These guys were in their mid- to late-thirties. They weren't 13-year-old boys dazzled by stardom (it would have been ridiculous for 13-year-olds to lead a safari). Their African contingent are a prominent reason why Arsenal are popular in the area. Some even like Emmanuel Eboue, while Kolo Toure can count on continent wide support. So, I reasoned, it wasn't all about success.

However, this is all enthusiasm that is unlikely to be repaid. Paul Kam's comments to me in China that United toured Asia to "reward" their fans would, if true, mean that clubs would come to Africa every summer given the enormous level of support. But, of course – whisper it mind – it's not about the fervour of support. It's really all about the money, and unfortunately for the likes of Kenya, in particular, hard cash is not something they can make available to global Premier League brands. Tourism remains a huge slice of their financial pie, generating around $1bn a year, more than horticulture and tea export combined, but riots following the 2007 elections have left the country struggling to recover its standing as a top destination. This fallout remains apparent with many people, driven from their homes by warring rival tribes, still living in UN refugee camps in the country.

Thinking on this, I wondered if this is all evidence to show that ultimately Asia is a lost cause for United. Penetration in Africa has been achieved, in part because of Premier League broadcasts, but because of a natural affinity for the game, it is inherent. The people here live and breathe football. It is their game, just as it is in Europe. It may come out in a love of English football, but the sport and watching it with friends is all culturally much closer to east African life than it is to Asian. The lack of facilities and infrastructure for everyone to have an HDTV and a digital satellite mean that here, more than anywhere, there is a natural need for people to congregate at the local pub to watch their football, but the depth of this commonplace access remains remarkable.

From Navasha we moved to the world-famous Masai Mara, where we spent two days on game drives, tracking animals in four wheel drive vehicles. It was a remote place – our camp was guarded at night by the Masai themselves – a place where you wake in the middle of the night to the sounds of Hyenas within the campsite itself, and can hear lions roar in the distance. It is as 'real' as nature gets and requires a set of skills to match. These were exemplified by our driver on the Mara, affectionately known as 'Big P', when he brought our six-man van to a shuddering halt in the middle of nowhere and simply said, "fresh dung". Minutes later we were the only van, in what was a surprisingly busy park, to be in the midst of a family of four elephants.

It is a place where bravery and honour have very different meanings (taking a last-minute, game-winning penalty is not amongst them), where the everyday sights for those from the Masai village are jaw-dropping experiences for us. Our highlight in that respect came early. On our first afternoon on the Mara, only our second game-drive in two weeks packed full, we were alerted to the presence of a dead cow in the park. It belonged to the Masai from the local village who bring their cattle to graze within the boundaries of the park when a lack of rain renders their ground barren. The cow had been killed by a lion, meaning, as I understood it, that the Masai were to leave the dead animal where it was or risk being arrested by the park rangers for disrupting the natural eco-system. But given the value of the animal to the village they weren't giving up that easily. While one of the villagers had returned in search of help, another, a boy of only around 13-years, remained to guard the body. As we made our way to the scene we stopped intermittently as lions were spotted in the undergrowth – exciting enough in itself. We sat in silent awe as one, two, three adults, with one, two, three, four youngsters slipped in and out of the grass, making their way to their stricken prey. Our van arrived with many others and the lions stopped, hiding in the undergrowth about 100 yards from the cow carcass. The Masai boy spread his bright red bodywrapping across the animal – years of conditioning means lions understand that the Masai red equates to danger – and grasped forlornly at his spear. This was a standoff, and the boy was not moving.

The trucks circled the area, some drivers trying to persuade the boy to give up the ghost and get inside a vehicle, but he clearly knew the value, even of a dead animal, to his village and was determined to stand his ground. A male lion, all glistening mane and strut, arrived on the scene and the pride edged closer, prowling, the tension mounting with every passing minute. The lions even used some of the vans as cover, but still they waited. The boy was unmoved, princely in his bravery, unperturbed, telling those who called out to him that he was not scared of the predators. I was, and I was in a van.

The pride moved as one, stalking, now only 30 yards away, and the boy eventually retreated to a van. But the presence of so many trucks clearly made the lions wary, and the cow was still swathed in red. The villagers returned to butcher the animal, asking us to leave out of respect. The vans drove away and the lions returned to the undergrowth. The boy's bravery had been richly rewarded.

We made a few passing returns to the site where the dismembered carcass and head of the cow remained; Jackal fodder we were told. As the park neared closing most people left, but Big P had something else on his mind. In what seemed like an idle last hour he circled the same bits of the park and when he returned to the site one final time only one other truck joined us. Vultures had begun to eat away at the carcass. A Jackal did turn up, but suddenly retreated as the pride of lions began their advance, slowly, gracefully, powerfully moving in stages. Two adult males played lookout as the three lionesses and four cubs moved in to rip apart the remainder of the cow. From ten feet away we witnessed the breathtaking sight and sounds of flesh being ripped and bones crunching. One of the best photos of our trip remains a lioness looking straight up at us in the top of our van, blood dripping from her mouth, a chillingly menacing quality to her eyes.

The almost mythic bravery of the boy to face down the pride and the ferocity that lurked behind the eyes of that lioness seemed a world away from what I had previous understood as reality.

Some of the group paid extra to glimpse inside this 'unreal' world with a trip to the Masai village (Clare had already done this on a previous trip, so we didn't go). I had already joked that we should take them a few red football shirts as it fitted the Masai's approach to style, and Steve, one of the guys I'd watched football with on the first night, told me on his return that as soon as they got to the gates of the village some of the children asked him whether he supported Manchester United or Liverpool and whether he had a spare shirt of theirs. He also reported that they'd been able to tell him the score of the Portsmouth match the previous night, and had likened another member of the group to Peter Crouch on account of his height. It appeared that the pub/post-office that we'd seen from the road also served as their football cinema, and was crammed full every time there was a Premier League match on. If that isn't rural penetration then I don't know what is – and all achieved without the need for biannual summer tours. Those Masai can jump too, so who knows what a United talent search might turn up. They'd certainly be better equipped than Jimmy Greaves to catch a stray dog. It was strange to share a similar frame of reference with such a different and distant world, although I doubt the 13-year-old boy protecting that cow was moved to wonder whether he should gamble a leg on Wayne Rooney scoring the first goal this coming weekend, or if Tevez was going to sign a permanent contract with the club, the current hot topic of conversation on the United internet forums.

English football's only rival for popularity, in Kenya at least, is Barack Obama. I knew they had a vested interest in the newly-elected President of the USA because of his Kenyan lineage, but Obama's image was the only challenge to the Premier League's presence in the country. Murals of him adorned walls, t-shirts were sold in every roadside stall, they'd declared a national holiday when he won the election and I'd even heard rumours of Barack Obama-branded paracetamol. We returned to Navasha for one night on the day of his inauguration and couldn't get into the bar, let alone get a seat. I could understand such a crush to watch the election results themselves maybe, but an inauguration? In such circumstances I had little hope of getting them to put the second leg of the semi-final of the Carling Cup on. The number of people had thinned out somewhat by the time I asked at the bar but the answer was negative. Thinking it was a brush off I mentioned that everyone in Kenya loves Obama and perhaps that was the reason. The barman said simply, "He gives us hope." Later he told me he was "born for Arsenal". Dramatic statements were obviously his forte.

I persisted. Although the bar was closing, and we had to get up at 6am the following day, I got them to search the channels again at kick-off time and they allowed me to sit in the outside bar area with a television long after they turned in for the night. A couple of others from the group stayed for the first half – which helped resolve a bill dispute with the bar manager, who after trying to lie about how many drinks we'd had merely said, "I can't tell, you all look the same" – but by the end I was on my own with only the distant noise of hippos yawning, an indescribably bone-shuddering sound, to scare the shit out of me.

That was the last of the games I got to watch under the huge, starlit African skies on safari. We caught the Everton game in a beachfront hotel on Zanzibar, where we stayed for our final three nights. On reflection three out of five matches watched was a hell of a lot better than the zero out of five I'd thought was likely. The two which I missed were out of my control. The first, the FA Cup game against Tottenham took place when we were in the middle of the middle of nowhere, staying on a campsite with one toilet, no electricity and seemingly nothing for miles. The Masai who stayed with us that night did have a radio by which they were listening to football, identifiable by the simple rise and fall of the commentary despite the language barrier, and through Pete I managed to establish that it was a local game. But later, even putting the radio at the top of a tree couldn't draw out the BBC World Service, and none of the local stations had opted to carry commentary of the game. It was the most cut-off from United we'd been and with no mobile reception either it wasn't until we'd driven for about three hours the following very early morning that I finally found out the score.

"Finding out results 12 hours late, you don't really like football anymore do you? What are you a casual fan?" Thanks Clare, just the support you can count on from a loved one.

The 5-0 thumping of West Brom came on our final night of camping, across the water from the Tanzanian capital, Dar es Salaam. The site had modern amenities, but a broken television and we were strongly advised against leaving the campsite to walk around an island devoid of any noticeable buildings. Despite the absence of facilities there were a few United shirts to be spotted the following day as we queued in the truck for the ferry back to the mainland, but my attempts to snap a few people in their kits provoked a hostile reaction and rocks were actually thrown at our van. One man threw a potato.

By the end of that day we were at a bar on the beach in Stone Town, Zanzibar, where a guy flogging postcards came to our table. After convincing him that we weren't buying anything he turned the conversation to Manchester United, and had an advantage over me, having seen the game the previous night.

"Oh he seems to be more of a fan than you, Tim!"

Guess who said that?

I asked him why he supported the club. His chosen material analogy was watches. "Why do you buy a good watch?" he asked rhetorically. "Take your watch," he began, but things fell flat when I proudly presented him my £11.99 Casio I'd bought specifically for travelling. As soon as it didn't sparkle, look outwardly impressive or better than other watches he wasn't interested. Maybe the east African fans weren't as loyal as I'd been trying to convince myself they were.

South Africa

OUDTSHOORN
West Ham (a) 1-0
UK time: 08/02/09, 16.00
Local time: 08/02/09, 18.00

'IF YOU'RE AN ostrich, this [Oudtshoorn] is the place to come for work.'

I'm not sure why a *Lonely Planet* writer would think an ostrich would be actively seeking work, or reading a guidebook for that matter, but who knows in Oudtshoorn. One of the towns easily accessible from Cape Town along Route 62, it is rightly called the ostrich capital of the world and could teach United a thing or two about brand-building. Now you might think, ok there's a few ostriches there and they make a big-deal out of it, but the town completely runs on the bird. The town emblem is an ostrich, naturally, there are opportunities to eat ostrich eggs (very rich) and ostrich meat in various forms – steak (nice) and sausages or meatballs (very nice) – while there are a couple of museums (rubbish) charting the history of the ostrich in both the town and across the world. Now you're probably wondering whether it featured Emu of Rod Hull fame? No, because Emu is, strangely enough, an Emu and thus just a relative of the ostrich. Finally, on every street corner there are people trying to flog you fans made of ostrich feathers or decorated ostrich egg shells.

We stayed for a couple of nights, one of which featured the United v West Ham game, as we sling-shotted from Cape Town and back again to be in the city for my brother's wedding at the end of the month. With the town being much bigger than others on the route, such as Montagu and Prince Albert, it seemed the best bet for a decent place outside of a big city to watch the football (the increase in price in accommodation in South Africa, compared to the likes of India, as well as hiring a car meant that rooms with TVs were once again beyond our financial grasp). That was the main attraction for me and I was interested to try the ostrich meat – but for Clare one thing stood out; the chance to ride an ostrich or, as I really knew it to be, the chance to watch me ride an ostrich.

So early one morning we drove out to Highgate Ostrich farm for a tour led by a sexually-repressed Congolese man, who managed to relate everything he showed us to "bedroom adventure" (this wasn't indicated on the flyer). He began by telling us that he was soon getting married to his girlfriend who he'd not seen for three years and that the union would finally enable him to fulfil his urges. Chuck in a tour that took in ostrich feathers, the consequent feather boas and the birds' incubation and breeding processes and you basically had a blueprint for *Carry on with the Ostriches*. Although, all this only proved a minimal distraction from the fear of what was to come.

We fed a couple of smaller ostriches, nearly losing a finger in the process, before our guide took us out to the riding spot. I'd thought that I might get away with it as I'd read there was some sort of weight limit, but he simply told me, "we just bring out the wild ones if we think it's necessary." I was avidly against riding an ostrich. I'd already nearly died riding a wild horse in Mongolia, so this just seemed reckless. Clare was also getting cold feet now the 'beasts' were up close and the tour guide had run through the gamut of ways they could kill you. But our host was giving us no choice as he saddled up a bird with what looked liked a tent's groundsheet and happily presented me with a "mad one". Brilliant.

I clambered on. "Sit back, sit back," they kept telling me. The idea is you have to grab hold where the wing meets the body; it feels pretty disgusting, a bit like putting your hands around a dead chicken. I grabbed on as tightly as I could.

"Put your feet together," was the next instruction and "steer with the neck," was the final cry as they ripped the mask off the ostrich's head, slapped it on the arse and off it shot. From then all I could hear was "keep you feet together" as my legs flailed out of control (I'm sure it kicked me at one point). There was, naturally, lots and lots of laughter, none of it from me. About 30 seconds later all they could hear was my best impression of a petulant eight-year-old: "I want to get off now. I don't like it. I want to get off," I squealed. Clare's ride was much smoother, unsurprising really given she rode something closer to a pheasant and one of the handlers walked slowly around behind it for the duration. She disputes this recounting of events, but tellingly we have a video of her ride but not mine because she said "it was just too fast to film". Fact. I was lucky to survive.

Watching the football was a damn sight easier than playing flightless bird bucking bronco. As we checked in I'd asked Marius, the owner, if he knew a pub I could watch the game in later. "Ah, playing West Ham aren't they?" he replied, noting a pub down the road that would potentially show it, but added: "I'll be watching it here, so you can watch it with me if you fancy it." The town seemed dead when we made a trip to the supermarket later and the ease with which he'd come up with the fixture had made me think he might be a United fan too, so his offer seemed as good as any. As it turned out when we returned to find him watching the north London derby in the communal area of the hostel, he was certainly into his football, but was in fact a West Brom fan. "How did that happen?" I asked.

"Well, I'm going to show my age. Just back in the 80s when we all got into football here, everyone just picked a team each. I picked West Brom." Not a bad choice back then, I thought – the early 80s having been glory days for the Baggies, with Big Ron at the helm and the Bryan Robsons of this world driving a powerful team forward. And at least he'd stuck by it, he had only 'picked' them in the first place, so could just as easily have changed.

As the game started Marius floated the idea that a United loss would at least make things more interesting in the league. I disagreed categorically. "Really?" he questioned and when he found out I actually went to games when at home, he said "Oh you're a real fan then, that's understandable." It was encouraging that he could make the differentiation between our respective levels of support and he highlighted that to this 'lower level' following, outside of England, the Premier League's strength of the competition and quality of the product, being far superior to South Africa's own football where long ball and dull matches abide, was all important.

I chatted to him over the course of the game and inevitably, as I was to find with any football discussion in South Africa, the attention switched to the 2010 World Cup, which he hoped would reach as far as the ostrich capital itself bringing an upturn for his business. It was interesting to get an inside take on the ticketing issues, that along with stadium construction and crime levels are the major challenges facing the country ahead of the tournament. It seems that while an outsider may assume, as I did, that cricket and rugby are the nation's biggest sports in terms of actual attendance figures, football is the most popular. The respective support that the three sports receive is divided along racial and financial lines and within football itself there is a similar split. South African football is attended, in the main, by the black and the less affluent population, who will ironically struggle to afford to attend World Cup matches, while the Premier League itself has become the football of the white and wealthier sections of society. This may feel like crass generalisation, but it is a surprisingly accurate summary of the situation that I didn't find anyone desperate to dispute.

Indeed, World Cup 2010 overlord Danny Jordaan even noted the trend during the 2009 Confederations Cup: "We have about 2.1 million football fans in this country who are white, but their teams are Manchester United, Liverpool and Chelsea. At the Confederations Cup they have really come out to support Bafana Bafana."

While in India a lot of the attraction of English football was a full stadium and an atmosphere absent from their own matches, here the reasons for the split between homegrown football and the Premier League were deeper-rooted socio-economic ones.

One thing not helping the English game, though, was the awful standard of punditry, exemplified by the commentators holding a five minute discussion on whether there would have been terracing or seating at Upton Park in the 1970s, ridiculous in its lack of appreciation of the pre-Premier game. I later witnessed an entire half-time devoted to explaining why a

Ronaldo header against Blackburn was disallowed. It was a blatant push, yet the three-man punditry team, former United keeper of the early 80s Gary Bailey included, decided that the audience needed to be treated to a full 15 minutes on it, with varying angles and exhaustive arrows to boot.

The on-screen punditry was a welcome distraction shortly into the second half when we were joined by a girl who, seemingly because she was English, was another who thought that she had to have some input into a football conversation.

"You know I've heard a rumour that if Man U win the league, especially if they win the quadruple, then Ryan Giggs will retire. Because it'll be the 11th and he's number 11." I mean, really.

"He's started discussions on a new contract I think," I offered (he actually signed an extension a week later).

"No, if they win it, that's the rumour I've been told." By who exactly?

"I don't believe that for a minute."

"No, it's definitely true." From rumour to true in five seconds. Why was she even saying this, for what possible reason other than to reveal her idiocy? This woman had just come from England; were they really considering a 'quadruple' back home? We weren't even through the second round of the Champions League yet, and were facing Jose Mourinho's Inter Milan in that, the league was looking like an inevitability at this stage, but three cup competitions? It seemed ridiculous.

Marius left around this point, pretending he had some work to do, but I think we all knew the real reason. He'd clearly enjoyed our football chat, and it was the game in general rather than United specifically that was enabling me to make connections here. A day later Clare went into the office to grab a drink while I just got in the car. She came out telling me I had to go in as Marius was looking for me. Phil Scolari had been sacked by

Chelsea a couple of hours previously and he'd been eager to get me that news. Football's ability to ice-break remains un-paralleled.

CAPE TOWN
Derby (h) 4-1
UK time: 15/02/09, 16.30
Local time: 15/02/09, 18.30

Fulham (h) 3-0
UK time: 18/02/09, 20.00
Local time: 18/02/09, 22.00

Blackburn (a) 2-1
UK time: 21/02/09, 17.30
Local time: 21/02/09, 19.30

Inter (a) 0-0
UK time: 24/02/09, 19.45
Local time: 24/02/09, 21.45

I'D BEEN TRYING to get a date with a Manchester United supporters' club for a while now. This particular quest had started back in Japan, but finally looked as though it was going to come to fruition in Cape Town. I wasn't sure how I felt about it. Obviously it would provide an easy one-stop-shop for meeting a group of United fans, presumably fairly opinionated and aware that I was coming. But at the same time these were the very organ-ised international brigades helping to create the problems I perceived in

United's global branding strategy and the consequent knock-on effects in the first place. Just to increase my trepidation, the first email that I received from them was signed off: 'glory, glory'. *Oh dear*, I thought, cringing just reading it.

My initial contact was a guy called Andrew Evans, and we were doing a great job of avoiding each other. We'd exchanged a few emails, so it made sense for me to go along to meet the group when he was there and would be confident of a decent turn-out. The first game during my stay, the Carling Cup semi-final second leg against Derby, was a non-starter, as Andrew was away with his girlfriend for Valentine's Day, an event they absolutely love in South Africa. So Clare and I took a chance on strolling up and down Long Street – Cape Town's major nightlife district – and came across an Irish pub to watch it in. The change of time zones, taking us to within just two hours of the UK, and the general feel of Long Street had made me confident enough to not do any research to find somewhere. We didn't have any problem locating a bar in which to watch the game, but hadn't bargained for being almost the only ones watching it. There had been some rugby on beforehand which had drawn quite a crowd, but for the duration of the United match there was little interest. People strolled in to check the score and give a little cheer, before making their way up Long Street, but no real support as such. *Where are the visible benefits of all these tours?* I thought.

The following match was my fault as I was out on my brother's stag-do in nearby Stellenbosch. Stellenbosch, a university town for rich kids from Cape Town best described as the perfect setting for a South African *Beverly Hills 90210*, is a famous stop in the wine-tasting region. Clare and I had visited it ourselves to take in some wineries and after picking up some maps, asked at the tourist information centre about the best way to get around as they didn't seem walkable. Drive was the answer. But how does that work with the actual tasting? We didn't know much about wine, so weren't going to compare vintages; we were going to drink some wine and eat cheese. "Well, we have rules for the roads in South Africa, but we don't really have any control over them, so driving is the best way. If you do get caught you will be in trouble, but . . ." Excellent advice from the national tourist board.

So we'd compromised; Clare ate cheese and I double-tasted wine for the day, and then we went out in the evening, dropping the car off at the hostel on the way.

Having taken a wrong turn at around 2am at the end of our night out, we were soon lost and went in search of directions from a security guard at a garage. He nonchalantly informed us that if we continued heading in the same direction we would be killed, and that instead he would call us a taxi. Ah, a taxi, a cut for him perhaps? "If you were serious about the danger, you'd call the police instead."

"Ok," he said and made a call on his mobile. This was supposed to be Stellenbosch, a safe haven amongst the reported heinous crime levels. Were we really in danger? It was noticeable that the guard's parting word to the person on the other end of the line was 'white'. The police soon turned up in a mini-van, with two seats upfront and a cage, evidently for any arrestees, at the back.

"We have a problem I think. We only have the two seats," one of the officers indicated.

"No we don't, we want to ride in the cage," Clare and I both said as we clambered towards our free taxi. *Stick to the beaten track* was the clear message when the officers dropped us off.

Back on Stellenbosch's beaten track for the stag night I attracted some derision when I took myself inside a pub for the Fulham match. But that was the reason we'd chosen that pub in the first place and, as I said to someone who complained, saying I should be outside with my brother, "he'd rather be in here watching this. You're the ones keeping him out there." It was true, although he displayed a remarkable capacity for walking in just as the goals were scored.

After the Blackburn game, which I caught on a television at our accommodation at the nearby Strand after saying farewell to members of my family who were flying home, it was time for the Inter Milan Champions League tie. This was the game I would watch with the supporters' club. It was only arranged at the last minute, as there had been some behind the scenes changes to make first. Obviously nine months previously a United v Inter Champions League tie was nowhere near planned and by sheer misfortune, and in the search for the cheapest route, our flight to New York was scheduled for the evening of the 24th. Had we stuck to it not only would I have missed the match, but a total flight time of 24 hours would have left me not knowing the score at all for a day. That was unthinkable.

"I think we've got a problem with one of our flights," I told Clare once the fixture date was confirmed.

"Again? What is it?" Our previous issue had arisen when our flight from Dar es Salaam was cancelled because the carrier, Air Tanzania, was grounded for safety breaches. Finding another for a decent price had been a bit of an ordeal.

"Well, the United…" I began.

"And you want us to move the flight?" She'd got there quickly enough.

"Oh, you know about it?"

"Well no, but you mentioned it might be close."

Pause.

"Just move it."

"Really? That easily? It'll cost £40."

"I'd rather pay £40 than have you squirming in the seat next to me on a plane for a day." And parents drum it into you for years that kicking up a fuss never helps you get your own way.

It was the first match on the trip that had cost us a direct payment outside of the night out. Clare's resignation was also interesting, in fact she hadn't really moaned about the games for a while now. On the day there was always a regular "I can't be bothered to go and watch this with you", but it was almost as though she said it for the sake of it, knowing it was no longer having an effect, as "come on, let's go" was my usual response.

Andrew Evans was called away for business at the last minute, and so wouldn't be there anyway, but put me in touch with another prominent member of the group, Sam Jones. I made arrangements to meet him at the pub on Cape Town's waterfront. I was nervous. This was a huge game, against one of what I saw as Europe's top three, away in Italy. For once I wasn't convinced we'd definitely win. It would be tense. Why had I chosen to put myself in a room full of strangers where I'd be expected to talk to them, discuss various aspects of the game, when really, if I was being honest, I'd already decided I didn't respect their opinions. The nerves would make my temper short, it always is for big games, so why had I allowed this match to be compromised in this way?

This supporters' group were a set of people feted by the club, given tickets for big games at the expense of others at home and courted during pre-season tours like those of 2006 and 2008. It went further than that, though, I discovered, once Sam and I started to talk. He had tales of meeting the team, the manager and knocking back tequilas with 1968 European Cup-winning legend Paddy Crerand. It was clear the club was on a charm offensive when abroad, using its assets to the max, and Sam clearly enjoyed it, just as I would have done. But what did we get back at home? An email saying: 'We think we're the best team in the world, we won some trophies last year and played pretty good football. You want a part of that again? Well you'll just have to pay a bit extra won't you? Oh yeah, and do it by this date or we'll flog your ticket and by the way you'll probably not notice things like a sliding scale for Champions League tickets so they cost you more just because we get further and of course you have to attend the reserve matches in the Carling Cup otherwise you ain't getting tickets to any of the finals. Yes, you can apply for away tickets, but don't think you'll be getting any. Considering not doing it? Come on don't be silly, we've got you over a barrel and we bloody know it.' It was the club that annoyed me with their attitude, not the supporters in Cape Town.

I asked the obvious question: why did they support the club? They avoided the success-ridden answers that I'd received up to now, but I didn't know whether they rang true. They were wary of my being there in some respects as some of the fanzines had been out there in the past and not been overly complimentary, so they were perhaps choosing their answers a little carefully. A number gave family as the reason (much of which didn't really stand-up to close examination such as grandparents from Wales and Ireland and parents who had supported the team because of links to the UK) and this did point to what was lacking in Asia; the generational effect. Did this mean that United could count on this support for years to come? I wouldn't go that far, but it was more assured than that in China, Japan or India.

The answers may have been a little different to what I expected but my overriding question was still 'what's the point?' It might be logical to point out they get access to the stars and the management when they tour

– but you could just turn out on the day for that, you didn't have to declare yourself a fan.

As kick-off neared, people continued to turn up in numbers. It was clear this was indeed a regular occurrence (Sam confirmed it wasn't for every game but was frequent) and the whole upstairs area soon filled. As a nervy game progressed, I observed the ebb and flow of the group and their constant interaction. People sat in separate clusters, but mostly they knew each other, or knew some other people there. It was a social event, like a mini-community; there was even a girl that all the younger lads fancied. It was, in a sense, like their own football ground, their own corner of the Stretford End, a small United community in Cape Town. Even to a doubter like me it was obvious what 'the point' was, it was clear why they did it. They'd hate me to say so, but the football was almost incidental. It was the lubricator of the event, the reason they were all here, but now it was established, now it was functioning, the football mattered little. That for me was the redeeming feature. Their gatherings, I learned, sprawled beyond the boundaries of the football season, with members of the group regularly meeting each other through the summer and on non-matchdays.

The game itself saw United play well, but fail to find the net and provide the necessary overwhelming relief of tension. The 'crowd' were trying their best to create an atmosphere – chanting, clapping, imploring – to make it feel real. Even when we chatted post-match, Sam was eager to impress on me the strength of their support with comments like: "It's a shame United didn't score, you didn't get to hear us cheer." It seemed those fanzine visits had made them warier than I'd thought and Sam was eager to point out the number of official shirts there were, describing at length the cost it took to get genuine items imported, having been annoyed that past articles had noted the tops were mainly fake. It was true the room was littered with genuine United merchandise, although that was more a point for the club to take heart from, not me, but he wanted to show they contributed in some way.

The post-match chat did again touch on the World Cup, indeed we were just down the road from Cape Town's Green Point stadium, and Sam accepted my theory about the division along racial lines and how ticketing would in all likelihood lead to the country's Premier League fans being the ones attending the World Cup matches. It almost felt that the 'Premier League' was a sport in itself, quite separate to South African football, with no specific loyalty to homegrown players like Benni McCarthy and Aaron Mokoena (both then at Blackburn). Although, I suspected that Lucas Radebe's fame and success at Leeds would have opened the Premier League door to the fans beyond this ilk.

The support was more English in its origin, but the social driver was the powerful element here, not an all encompassing concern over the future of the club. Sam's response to my questioning him about the Glazers issue was that "it seems ok, though" and when I tried to impress on him that a year or two without Champions League football would in all probability be fatal, he couldn't see that we wouldn't play in the competition so, naïvely in my opinion, wasn't concerned. Would the support here stand up to any slump in the club's fortunes? Who knows? They, naturally, maintained it would, and the social side might just be enough to keep things together anyway. I'm not sure poor quality football alone would.

While the way the club courted this enclave of fans angered me, and the lack of concern over the two watchwords of 'Glazer' and 'ticketing' was telling, it would be churlish to think that the use of football as a social lubricator wasn't a wholly uplifting one and I had again enjoyed myself. Perhaps I was gaining new perspectives on the reasons for and the rights and wrongs of support? Maybe football isn't merely about the, well, the football. Maybe that was a problem with the English mindset. After all, it was that which was causing me to rally against this fringe support in the first place. However this attitude existed in the South Africa psyche too. Sam told me that upon informing people that he was a United fan in Cape Town, they'd often respond with that familiar shrug: "not another Man United fan", ludicrous given their own affiliation to another Premier League club, usually, as he pointed out, Liverpool.

Sam has now moved to England and believes the anti-United attitude is stronger here (I was surprised it existed at all in South Africa), and while in what I believed to be true fan fashion he moved to allow him to be closer to the club and attend matches on at least a semi-regular basis, it is the chance to meet his old friends at the supporters' club on the Waterfront in Cape Town that he misses above all else.

Perhaps I'd read the situation correctly after all. It seemed meeting these United fans and searching out the matches was allowing me, in fact Clare as well, to learn about the nature of the people in each country and explore new parts of the places themselves. I was certainly gaining more of an insight than any trip to the top of Table Mountain could provide, although the view from the pub wasn't as good.

USA

NEW YORK CITY

Spurs (n) 0-0, won on pens
UK time: 01/03/09, 15.00
Local time: 01/03/09, 10.00

Newcastle (a) 2-1
UK time: 04/03/09, 19.45
Local time: 04/03/09, 14.45

Fulham (a) 4-0
UK time: 07/03/09, 17.15
Local time: 07/03/09, 12.15

"HOW LONG HAVE you been waiting in that queue, about two, two-and-a-half hours?" the immigration official asked.

"About three."

"Yeah sorry about that. You were just unlucky."

"Right."

"You got caught up in that double-decker Emirates plane that just landed from Abu Dhabi and you don't want to get caught up in that."

"Right." *Just put me through,* I thought.

"You see all the people on that plane are called Mohammed, and when you consider that 90 per cent of all the people called Mohammed are wanted by the FBI then it's going to take a while."

"Oh."

"Anyway, you're through, welcome to America." Great. Living in America...

I had mixed feelings about going to America from a footballing point of view. From a travelling perspective I thought it would provide a good end to our trip; a chance to be entertained, after a lot of sightseeing, for as long as our money lasted. I'd always tried to avoid subscribing to the notions that Americans are fat, stupid and very often both, but the welcome at JFK didn't exactly get things off on the right foot.

However, we were in New York and it was fantastic, if not a little cold. Plunging from the 37 degrees of Cape Town to the minus 4 of the Big Apple, all without a coat, was a bit of a shock. Having spent the first day buying the required coats and then gloves, and then a hat and then some boots, as the temperature dive-bombed to minus eight and snow blanketed the city, we were ready to go and watch the Carling Cup final the following morning.

Following the Cape Town success, I'd decided to contact the American branch of the official supporters' club, expecting New York to be one of its main haunts. Although it was, they lacked the communal meeting policy of Sam and Co., but the group's leader identified the Red Lion pub as his venue of choice. The game was to kick-off at 10am; we were staying in the Upper West Side of Manhattan and had to get to Greenwich Village. It was all so *Sex and the City*, all I needed now was to get a friend that looked like a horse and 'get to thinking'. After negotiating a few Sunday Metro alterations, we arrived at about 9.30am to find most people were feeling like we did. Inside the very dark bar – a common theme in New York where daylight seems forbidden from most drinking establishments – people sat quietly sipping tea and coffee. There wasn't much beer to be seen, it was clearly far too early for a football match.

The crowd appeared to be mainly English, but for the first time I could recall on the trip wasn't hugely slanted in United's favour (admittedly sometimes there had just been me watching but that still represented a 100 per cent swing). There were plenty of Tottenham fans. However, the atmosphere was just plain flat. The game was dull, but even when it went to penalties things didn't really get going and it was a disappointing way to watch the final, particularly when I knew there was a ticket with my name on it (literally) across the Atlantic. I had actually hoped for the atmosphere of Delhi or Cape Town, but I got nothing like that. The only people to raise more than a whisper were a couple of 'Yanks' just to the side of us who, perhaps significantly, were even starting to annoy Clare (who displayed more demonstrable ability to identify players than they did) with their facile comments. With their "Gibbos" and "Fossies", their berating Ben Foster one minute before describing him as a "ledge" – it was the kind of idiocy that would have been expected from the Tim Lovejoy brigade.

It was the attitude I'd been worried about encountering. The Americans that had been in the pub for the Arsenal game in Cambodia had a similar way about them, while another of Uncle Sam's finest that I'd met in Siberia enthusiastically announced that he supported "Manchester" because of "Tevez, I just love that guy". For every story I've come across on the trip of Asia's passion for the game, there's been one for America's disinterest, but perhaps worse still are those Americans who take an interest but just don't get it. The story of a section of the crowd whooping at a long Gary Neville throw-in on the tour back in 2003 remain unforgettable in that respect. Perhaps this obnoxious, over-exuberant attitude was quietening the English voices further.

I thought New York might be different, possibly the saving grace of America. United had focused on the city in some respects; signing a deal with the New York Yankees back in 2001 for the purposes of selling themselves as a package to potential sponsors and to facilitate the sharing of 'insider' marketing information from either side of the Atlantic. Presumably United were able to tell the Yankees that there was 'no interest' in them in the UK, while the Yankees could tell United that there was surprisingly 'no interest' in them in the US, all top secret stuff. The Yankees have, of course, managed to sell a few baseball caps over the years in England, so perhaps this is behind the appearance of United hoodies and zip-up tops in highstreet clothing stores like Urban Outfitters in New York. The idea of a football team as a 'fashion' brand was a new thing. I'd been told the game as a whole was a 'fashion' or 'fad' in the big Asian cities, but this was a new spin, trying to trade on the badge as an iconic image, although surely pushing the suggestion that the club is merely a fashion accessory is hardly the way to engender long-lasting support?

In the grand scheme of things it's small fry, let's be honest. America is a crowded market place for sport anyway, where whooping and hollering rule and football is simply not going to take off – and if the people that are following the game are going to be quite so intolerable then I honestly don't care what they think about it.

The following Wednesday, when United faced Newcastle in the middle of the afternoon, we sought out another venue closer to where we were spending the rest of the day. It was a pub that billed itself as: 'Nevada Smiths – where Football is Religion. The Planet's most famous live Football venue. Experience the legendary matchday atmosphere in the place the hardcore call the Church.'

Quite a boast to live up to.

Old Trafford, the Camp Nou, the Maracana, the San Siro, Gigg Lane, Nevada Smiths: spot the 'Planet's most famous live Football venue'. Understandably I wasn't looking forward to it; by now I just wanted to be able to watch the games in my usual environment. True, I was really enjoying myself in New York as a visitor but I was just growing tired of the charade that watching United was becoming. I was finding moments of enjoyment in it, but they were small consolation. I wanted, needed to be back at Old Trafford.

The attempted Americanism of the game embodied by the over-the-top claims of Nevada Smiths only exacerbated this feeling. The match itself actually turned out to be quite enjoyable and the pub was rammed with fans from around the world as a selection of games from different European leagues were broadcast all around the bar. I asked a guy to the side of me why he supported United: "because they rock, dude," was his one-line response. I didn't ask him to confirm whether he'd ever heard *Come on You Reds*.

In front of us stood two Americans who, for the first two hours, supported United in the most vocal way possible, before switching immediately to Barcelona the moment their game replaced ours. It looked like a pick 'n' mix approach to fandom. I asked them which team they supported.

"Manchester United from England, Barcelona from Spain," was the reply. What was the point in that? The two are deadly rivals in the Champions League. It was strange, it made football lose any sense of place.

Why was it that the whole thing was quite so irritating? Was it simply because the two nations are so culturally different? It's incorrect to assume that we are really all that close to our American cousins just because of a shared language and political backslapping. These only go to hide a huge chasm between us. The whole bravado of Nevada Smith's self-proclamations, the whole just selecting the best team in each country, the whole "because they rock"; none of it appealed. In fact I found it downright repulsive because it was trying to put an American slant to what, to me, remains a wholly English sport. We might have a league littered with foreign stars, but the culture of football watching, the culture of fandom, is the strongest part of the English game's identity and trying to change that causes problems. That's why foreign owners face such resistance in England where foreign players are only seen to enrich the league. It is this aggressive commercialisation as much as the debt that I fear as a United fan with the club under the Glazers' direction. The whole 'Glazer-dome' might be a bit far fetched, but the 'best club in the world' tags, and the cringe-worthy pre-match announcements that "we as a club have the vision to be the best in the world both on and off the field", smack of American hyperbole and that will never sit well with the match-going regulars – but then what do they matter these days?

Surely if football is to work in the States then it will be the MLS, catered to the cultural facets of the country that will succeed. The very nature of their sport itself is just so different. Yes it's in the scorelines, in the emergency added on overtime to avoid a draw at all costs, but it's the affectations of support that are remarkably unique. After the United v

Newcastle game, we headed to Madison Square Garden to watch the New York Knicks take on the Atlanta Hawks. The change in atmosphere was astonishing, going from the pub with a heavy English slant to the crowd to the all-American ambience of the basketball arena.

I was looking forward to the basketball. I wasn't expecting it to be the same as football, that was kind of the point of it being a different sport, but I was amazed at how insipid it felt. I'd watched basketball on television in its UK hey-day on Channel 4 and found it fairly enjoyable. It had always seemed the epitome of American sport, almost an athletic Hollywood, if you will, with that very glitz and glamour turning heads away from football in China. Turns out that's right in many respects, as basketball is the only sport I think I've seen that's better on television than live. The constant scoring doesn't generate more excitement, in fact it only dilutes the tension. But the problems this creates that can be seamlessly papered over on the television, where motor-mouth commentary and great direction weaved together beautifully, are only exacerbated at a live game which cannot be bound together with the same fluency. The consequent impact this has on the crowd cannot be underestimated.

There's just no intensity to the event. People come and go, and in all honestly barely seem to care until the last few minutes as the consistency of scoring robs the game of any palpable sense of urgency until then. The 'audience' chat, they go in and out every five minutes for food, and they applaud; some every time there's 'a score', others when something a bit more out of the ordinary happens. It's so formulaic and repetitive (apart from when they do things like taking the players off court to run a promotion) that there's just no edge to it. There's no feeling that if you blink you might just miss an absolutely unforgettable moment of grace and skill. Yes, this was my first live basketball game, but it doesn't take an expert in a particular sport to understand the culture of the crowd, and that is where football wins out. That's why commentators on tennis and cricket constantly resort to saying 'it's like a football crowd out there.' Basketball was just so sanitised and lacked any sort of punch.

If United games lose their intensity and the unique culture and ideals of supporting the club become further diluted by packs of fans from the four corners of the world, then the crowd will cease – and many would say it already has – to be one living breathing organism representative of a set of values, shared on some level. It would become that very style of 'entertainment' that it just isn't, that it shouldn't be, and once that happens then it can be freely exported around the world with no noticeable impact. It would be no different to a Kylie Minogue world tour. Aside from a lack of hot-pants now Ronaldo has left.

Nevada Smiths did have the right sort of atmosphere to an extent (a guy in a Liverpool shirt standing in the middle of the bar cheering on United's opposition wouldn't really wash in England) so we returned for the Fulham FA Cup game to see United play the kind of slick attacking football of the previous season. It was a decent match in a decent atmosphere, and was a good one to end our New York stint on. It's a thoroughly enjoyable city that seems able to avoid much of what makes America rub people up the wrong way, but can't quite break free of what makes American sport American and stop people shouting 'shoot-it' during football matches. The other side of the country seemed unlikely to get any better.

CALIFORNIA (AND VEGAS)

Inter (h) 2-0
UK time: 11/03/09, 19.45
Local time: 11/03/09, 12.45 (Vegas)

Liverpool (h) 1-4
UK time: 14/03/09, 12.45
Local time: 14/03/09, 05.45 (Vegas)

Fulham (a) 0-2
UK time: 21/03/09, 15.00
Local time: 21/03/09, 08.00 (Anaheim)

Villa (h) 3-2
UK time: 05/04/09, 16.00
Local time: 05/04/09, 08.00 (Yosemite)

Porto (a) 2-2
UK time: 07/04/09, 19.45
Local time: 07/04/09, 11.45 (Fresno)

Sunderland (a) 2-1
UK time: 11/04/09, 15.00
Local time: 11/04/09, 07.00 (Beatty)

Porto (a) 1-0
UK time: 15/04/09, 19.45
Local time: 15/04/09, 11.45 (LA)
Everton (n) 0-0, lost on pens

UK time: 19/04/09, 16.00
Local time: 19/04/09, 08.00 (Palm Springs)

Portsmouth (h) 2-0
UK time: 22/04/09, 20.00
Local time: 22/04/09, 12.00 (Santa Monica)

BY THE TIME we got to California I was jaded. I'd wanted to search out these United fans yes, but primarily I was there as a fan of the team. I wanted to get an enjoyment out of my football and that was being compromised. I was still getting pleasure from the travelling, but it got to the point where I was honestly finding the football, on a week-by-week basis, a pain in the arse. I desperately wanted to go home to be at Old Trafford as the season climaxed, but yet stay travelling as long as I could.

There were highs (betting one day's budget on United to beat Inter in a Vegas casino and winning, which suddenly made Clare a bit more interested in the result) and hard-hitting lows (getting up at 5.45am and losing 1-4 at home to Liverpool was spectacularly deflating, before having to drive five hours to San Diego. Being out of the way of a media that would go to town on the debacle was small consolation). But generally it was a slog. The seven, later eight-hour time difference meant a lot of early mornings before bars opened, watching games live streamed on stuttery internet connections on my own, while Clare slept. It was clear that these two parts of my life, United and travelling, were finally heading for a collision.

We knew we had to head home relatively soon as our money was running out. So, we decided to sign-off in style by going to the Coachella festival near Palm Springs (although speaking of sanitised American experiences this was no festival in the traditional sense, with beer pens for drinking and $300 camping packages) and that would be that, seven months over in a flash. The end of the trip and its impending conclusion was never really far from our thoughts after our penultimate flight (New York to Vegas) was out the way. Knowing I was coming back to a fairly decent line-up of games with Tottenham, Arsenal and City all at home and potentially two more Champions League rounds to play only had the effect of making things worse every time I got up early, on my own, and quietly sat at the computer wearing headphones, watching a game.

The travelling was still great; two days of Masters Series Tennis in Indian Wells, a visit to Universal Studios, a road trip up the Route 1 coast-line to San Francisco – driving over the Golden Gate Bridge, visiting Alcatraz (on the same boat as Martin Keown and family) – and three days of camping in Yosemite national park amongst the highlights.

Yosemite provided perhaps the most interesting of the games we watched during this time. The temperatures may have dropped low enough at night (minus four) for me to label some of my clothes as my 'sleeping trousers and jumper', and had we not had our own sleeping bags in addition to the blankets provided for us then we may well have frozen, but we still managed to force our way out of bed at 7am to head for the warmth of the café where we were going to try and watch the Villa home game.

I'd spoken to the bar manager the night before and spent about 30 minutes flicking through the channels with him (after waiting until the semi-final of the college basketball championships had finished – the only sporting event Americans had seemed interested in since we landed in Vegas) to determine they had the Fox Soccer Channel. There was a television in an open seating area that he said I could get switched on the following morning if I spoke to one of the duty-managers.

When we got inside the warmth, Clare headed off to get us some tea – it never failed to be a little bit embarrassing, throughout our time in the States, to follow someone who had just ordered a frocca-chocca-mocca-skinny-latte with chocolate, no cream but soya milk and froth, by asking for "two cups of tea please" – and I went in search of a manager. I couldn't find one.

I explained the situation to one of the guys in charge of seating in the main canteen area and although he looked at me strangely he dispatched a colleague to look for the missing manager. She appeared a few minutes later and I was ready to explain my strange fascination with the sport to her but the seating guy chose to introduce me with, "this gentleman wants the television on."

"Oh," was her understandable reaction. I wasn't going to check out waterfalls, go hiking and avoid bears during my time in Yosemite. No, I wanted the television on. Federico Macheda announced himself to the world just under two hours later, but aside from my exuberant cheering leading to a member of staff asking, "what's going on here then?", the strangest occurrence came slightly before that. Clare had managed to miss most of the goals as usual, and had just returned from a toilet-break (that had seemingly induced Ronaldo's equaliser) when Danny Welbeck had a gilt-edged chance saved by Brad Friedel. As my hands went to my head in dismay, Clare lunged forward slightly, a lunge I'd seen before. It was the kind of uncoordinated slow motion head lunge perfected by Sir Alex Ferguson himself. The kind that has been seen countless times on the touchline as United create a chance in the closing stages of a tight game, a lunge with which he significantly tries to will the ball over the line.

"I saw that by the way," I ventured at the end of the game.

"Saw what?"

"You know that little jump, that lunge you did when Welbeck had that chance."

"You saw nothing."

"You were bothered about the result."

"No I wasn't."

"Yeah, you better not be."

"Tim, I hate football."

"Good."

Clare has known since we met that she's had some investment in the result, not because she was interested in the success of the team, but, as is the case with many a football widow, she knows its ability to shape my mood. But this season she'd actually had to watch matches, admittedly any that didn't provide her an opportunity to drink she usually slept through, but it remained a departure from the norm. It could have had worrying consequences.

Her indifference to Ronaldo's 35-yarder in the quarter-final of the Champions League in Porto suggested it wasn't necessarily an ongoing concern. In an LA pub, mainly dominated by Arsenal fans watching their own quarter-final, the differences in viewing culture were rammed home once again by Gunners and United fans wishing each other good luck (that wouldn't happen at home, although I guess a potential semi-final between the two would make a better atmosphere in such a pub when going to the ground is not a concern). Equally the ubiquitous and annoying shouts of "shoot-it" were joined by those asking for a quick "transition".

I hated watching football here. I didn't care what the American fans thought and they didn't give a toss what I or anyone else had to say. I canvassed a variety of opinions from those watching and from members of the American branch of the supporters' club from across the country, to see if there was any difference, but tellingly most (there were at least some dissenting voices) answers were of the same ilk.

On the Glazers, on the occasions that the conversation didn't just stop at the mention of their name, the consensus was: no problem with the ownership, they're businessmen, they keep giving to the transfer budget. Even pushing on these lines, deliberately leading people to be critical, couldn't elicit a negative comment. I was sick of it.

On ticketing: "ticket prices have gone up yes but that doesn't affect me so I'm not too concerned." "Ticket prices are still lower than some other top clubs and some that don't have as much success." "It's business, it's not the Glazers' fault." Why weren't these people concerned by these things – when have ticket prices ever been linked to success? Ticket prices in London should be higher, that's what salary weightings are for. Prices should reflect the cost of living, not exploit success.

They just didn't really care about the fans as a whole. While I was on the west coast, a whole group of them had travelled over to Manchester for both the Inter and Liverpool home games and I guess if you only have to pay for tickets twice, and they are arguably two of the biggest games of the season then you're not really going to care. It was a selfish attitude that made them part of the club, not a part of the fans that make the club. I wasn't asking for them to form a picket line outside the ground, all I wanted was some appreciation of the issues important to regular match-goers and those bound up in the club's history and culture. If you can't get that from the 'fans' then you're fighting a losing battle. I soon came to understand that I wasn't going to get anywhere. I could talk until I was blue in the face, but it would simply make no difference. America was the country that I'd thought would be easiest to travel around because I assumed it'd have the most similarities with the UK. However, for the first time, exploring United's fanbase actually made me feel more detached from and disinterested in the place we were visiting.

I was counting down the games until the Tottenham one now – the first one I would watch in the flesh for over six months – ticking them off. The last match of our trip, against Portsmouth, finally arrived. I sat on the mezzanine level of the Britannia Pub in Santa Monica (Clare had gone to park the car and I'd jumped out because we were running late). I was the only one up there until a local came up.

"Oh brilliant – soccer! I love soccer, it's my favourite," he said. I ignored him, he looked a bit dodgy. "Hey man, I love soccer." Oh god, what's this.

"Good," I replied, as a bartender came up the stairs.

"Do you want to order some drinks or food?" the waiter asked me.

"In a minute maybe, I'm just waiting for someone."

"And you sir?" to the other guy.

"No, I'm waiting for someone too." No, you're not, you've just copied me. The bartender nodded and returned downstairs.

"Hey man, do you want a bet?"

"No thanks. I just want to watch the match."

"Oh, ok. How about you just give me five bucks then?"

Here we go. . . "Sorry, no."

"One buck?"

"Sorry I can't, I'm going home tomorrow, so I've only got a little bit left."

"Alright then." And off he shot. There was simply no money in him trying to pretend he liked football. Sound familiar?

ENGLAND (and ROME)

Tottenham (h) 5-2

Arsenal (h) 1-0

Middlesbrough (a) 2-0

Arsenal (a) 3-1

Man City (h) 2-0

Wigan (a) 2-1

Arsenal (h) 0-0

Hull (a) 1-0

Barcelona (n) 0-2

WE ARRIVED HOME late on Friday 24 April. On Saturday, I dragged my heavily jet-lagged body to the Tottenham match – but it wasn't remotely a struggle. It felt like the first game of the season. I was eager; I couldn't wait for the action to start. It didn't matter what game it was, it didn't matter what stage of the season it was, I was genuinely surprised by just how excited the game was making me. It wasn't wholly a product of the length of time since I'd been to a match, it was the elation of going after missing-half a season that I should have been at, multiplied by the conditions in which I'd been watching those I'd missed.

I was happy that I felt like this. It was all about the wonder of going to see a United game, the headiness of just being there and watching the football. It disassociated it from success – it was the act that was important. Admittedly, 2-0 down at half-time wasn't great, and it was no surprise that my brother turned to me and offered a fantastic welcome home: "this is your fault. You shouldn't have come back."

"No . . . *that* was my fault," was my handy reply as the result swung to 5-2 in United's favour in the second half. This was not the length and breadth of our conversation on that day, obviously, but it was pretty much all football-related chat. It made it clear how much I really had missed by not going to the games. It's all the small things that make a match individual, that mark it out as particular and make it memorable – all the aspects you just can't get from a television. As he ran me through the this-happeneds and that-happeneds, both on and off the pitch, I came to realise that I'd missed a lot, much more than I realised. Even the weather can shape the experience – as I'd missed out on the League Cup tie with QPR and headed off for some drinks in Siem Reap, he'd been at Old Trafford in freezing temperatures with empty seats surrounding him, weighing up whether he should stick it out if the game went to extra-time. This made me appreciate that although I'd been watching the games (I had managed to see 39 of the 47 while I was away), I wasn't really connected to the action, I wasn't really 'in the know' for the duration of my trip. And that was after missing just seven months. If I'd never even set foot outside of the continent of Asia then what hope of connection would I have had?

That perhaps was *it* then. I hadn't really comprehended it up to now, but on returning to watch United I understood it in one fell swoop. I knew I'd lost out by not being there, but I didn't know the specifics of what I was missing out on. Now that I did it felt a lot worse than I'd previously thought. Maybe that was why fans across the world didn't think there was a real difference in supporting from Africa on television or at Old Trafford; they hadn't been in the position to appreciate what they were missing. It's better to have loved and lost . . . but my experience taught me it's not better to have gone to the football on a regular basis and then have that taken away from you.

I'd spent the last seven months trying to rationalise things to attempt to understand why people supported the club. I could see why it happened, and the reasons for it continuing, but now, returning to the ground and going to the game, I realised more than ever that being a fan so removed from the action or the culture of the club was even more pointless than I'd ever imagined. Sacrificing the chance to watch live sport at home for the televised spectacle made even less sense.

The football was fantastic and, although I got used to it again, I wasn't taking any part of it for granted. Not all went well, either. Financially ruined by our trip I had to scrape together (i.e. borrow) the money to get to Rome to see what in basic terms amounted to the biggest match that the club had ever lost. The 2-0 defeat to Barcelona in the Champions League final was a horribly deflating end to the season. My one chance to really revel in the glory of the campaign shot down in flames (the presentation of the league title felt undeniably flat). There was no anger because of the loss, no feelings of being cheated, not really any feelings of being outplayed. It felt entirely our fault and for that reason it knocked the wind well and truly out of me.

Did I feel any less affected because of my seven months away? Hard to say for certain obviously, but I doubt it.

That I'd missed most of the season and then turned up for the Champions League semi-final, final and a couple of plum league games did in a way make me hypocritical, yes. But as I said at the outset that's part of the game for a football fan, and I was hardly likely to give up my ticket because of my conscience was I? That was the crux of the matter though, the fight between logical rationalisation and being a football fan.

Had the trip given me a new perspective on supporting United? I understood why the likes of Rahul did so, and appreciated the life-affirming social benefits for Sam and Co., and I realised the facile nature of lambasting a poverty-stricken Cambodian for following the side. So yes, yes it did. But only on reflection. Ask me the same question without consideration and the instinctive reaction was, *what's the point?* Why? Because being a football fan and being rational don't really go hand in hand.

Perhaps it's just too easy to declare oneself a Manchester United fan. Maybe there should be a 'fit and proper persons' test for such things, looking at a combination of heritage, commitment, knowledge, genuine desire and other such facets. You know, maybe they should cut people and see if they bleed red . . . but how can you ever get to the point where you can decide who does and doesn't *deserve* to be there (or even simply be a supporter for those who do not go to the match)?

If my trip revealed anything to me it was that this dilemma remains an English disease. The psyche of the football supporter is such an intrinsic part of any particular country's make-up, an expression of a nation's individual traits, that it was never going to produce a set of shared ideals – either in what generates support or how that support is expressed. Perhaps in such a small world it is the ideals of a sports fan today that truly capture cultural divides, differences and idiosyncrasies.

The very nature of this discussion does seem quintessentially English though, and maybe it's not just restricted to football. Soon after we got back home we visited Clare's sister's house and Clare mentioned one of her friends was going to watch Take That the following night. Clare's sister went mental, going on about how she didn't deserve to go, how she hadn't been a fan the first time around, and was just jumping on the bandwagon; ultimately the point was, of course, that the upshot of these nouveau-boy band fans was that she hadn't been able to get tickets herself. "Maybe you should write a book about it," I suggested.

As for me? If anything, the whole adventure only hardened my support. You wouldn't expect me to say anything else, would you? But it's true. And Clare? Well, she hasn't watched a minute of football since we got home.